SEEKING CHRISTMAS

Finding Testimonies of Christ
in the Symbols and Traditions of Christmas

LARRY AND LISA LAYCOCK WITH RYAN AND LARISSA CHASE

Text copyright © 2016 Larry and Lisa Laycock

Cover and interior design by Mark Sorenson, copyright © 2016 by Covenant Communications, Inc.

Cover image: *Three Christmas Candles* © FCA Foto Digital

Published by Covenant Communications, Inc.

American Fork, Utah

Printed in the United States of America

First Printing: October 2016

22 21 20 19 18 17 16   10 9 8 7 6 5 4 3 2 1

ISBN-13: 978-1-52440-120-7

TABLE OF CONTENTS

INTRODUCTION

The Apostle Paul teaches that all things bear witness of the profound love and amazing grace of our Savior, Jesus Christ: "That in *every thing* ye are enriched by [Jesus Christ], in all utterance, and in all knowledge; Even as the testimony of Christ was confirmed in you" (1 Corinthians 1:4–6, emphasis added).

Our loving Heavenly Father states: "All things have their likeness, and all things are created and made to bear record of me, both things which are temporal, and things which are spiritual; things which are in the heavens above, and things which are on the earth, and things which are in the earth, and things which are under the earth, both above and beneath: all things bear record of me" (Moses 6:63). All things testify of both Heavenly Father and Jesus Christ for the reason that Jesus is the perfect emulation of our Heavenly Father.

Is it really possible that *everything* can enrich us by confirming our testimony of Jesus Christ?

Many years ago, our family decided to spend an entire Christmas season experimenting on this principle. Through our holiday experience, we learned that everything in the celebration of Christmas truly does have the power to enhance our belief in Jesus Christ.

Our experiment began when Larry tried a legal case that took him away from home for several months. During that time, he was only able to return home for a short stay each weekend. Needless to say, between church and family responsibilities, time for family fun and recreation diminished drastically, and our family was strained.

Finally, in September of that year, he completed his case and returned home to stay. He wandered around the house, feeling lost at first, but soon he commenced busily preparing our Christmas decorations.

What? Dad is doing Christmas stuff in September? Little by little, Christmas appeared all over our house. Using my most artful diplomacy, I (Lisa) tried to persuade him that it would not be a good idea to decorate our entire house and put up our Christmas tree until we were a little further into the Christmas season, but he persuasively argued: "I need to *feel* Christmas right now!"

"Feeling Christmas" is what Christmas is all about. The anticipation of the holiday season is a magical feeling that unifies families and friends, and creates hope and peace in a troubled world.

That year, our family gathered together on a cool autumn evening in the glow of our Christmas tree lights and "felt Christmas." We read the Nativity story together. Although it was only September, our reading served us well, helping us to focus on the Spirit of Christ very early in the holiday season. Our Nativity reading inspired us to plan and look for precious opportunities to honor Christ by serving others. We decided that we would conduct an experiment to determine for ourselves whether or not *everything* about Christmas really can confirm our testimony of Christ.

Months later, after that holiday season had become a sweet memory for all of us, we frantically gathered our family one July evening, exclaiming that we were facing a huge family emergency. Concern furrowed Larry's brow as he quietly looked us all in the eyes and said, "Christmas is coming!" He then smiled as he explained that he wanted us to continue the tradition we had begun the previous Christmas. He wanted us to carefully plan and prepare to seek Christ in Christmas every Christmas for the rest of our lives. And he invited us to commit to do that.

Over the years, we have kept our commitment and maintained our sweet tradition. Each year, we gather our family early in the season to read the Nativity story and look for secret, special ways we can serve others and, in doing so, become more like our Savior. Our children have fond memories of these events, and now they incorporate variations of our Nativity reading experience and our Christ-seeking activities in their own homes. We continue to believe that everything around us truly does have the power to testify of our Savior.

Our experiment forever changed the way we celebrate Christmas by deepening our belief in our Savior and His power to transform us into better people. Through this book, we will share insights and activities to help you and your family seek Christ in Christmas.

Even Santa Claus, Christmas stockings, gingerbread, and mistletoe bear record of Jesus Christ. When we actively seek Christ in Christmas, we can find testimonies of Him in all of our traditions, customs, and keepsakes. These precious testimonies will enhance our relationships, fill our hearts with charity, and teach us how to become more like our Savior.

CHAPTER 1

THE CHRISTMAS SEASON

HOW DOES THE CHRISTMAS SEASON CONFIRM OUR TESTIMONY OF CHRIST?

The Christmas season bears record of Jesus Christ and His doctrine that the family is ordained of God. As a vital part of our Christmas celebration, we honor the traditional human family by celebrating the miraculous birth of Jesus Christ into a holy family. We think of the majesty of His life and teachings, and we gather with family and loved ones in the hopes of strengthening family ties. The very spirit of the Christmas season whispers to us of the rich meaning of eternal life and the teachings of Jesus Christ—through Him, we can be saved from sin and physical death, and because of Him, we can be together with our families forever.

For many, the mere mention of the word *Christmas* evokes memories of home, happiness, and family that emerge in a wonder of joyful sights, sounds, and smells. We envision family togetherness with drifting snow and warm firelight; we breathe the aroma of freshly baked cookies, and we hear sweet melodies of hope. Waiting and wanting come to an end. In the birth and life of Christ, we find contentment, satisfaction, and completion, for everything good is gathered in Him, and all of the sights, smells, and sounds of the Christmas season focus our thoughts on Him and His divine plan of happiness for the human family. The Christmas season is the perfect time to fit our feelings for heaven, as we focus them upon our families. We can decide to seek Christ in our celebration of Christmas as we choose to allow the enchanting spirit of Christmas to change us for the better, to heal our hearts, and to strengthen the bonds of our family relationships.

Serving as mission president and companion in Chile, we taught many people that the family is ordained of God and is the most important social unit in time and eternity (see *Preach My Gospel*, lesson 1, concept 2). We know that if we foster family relationships and live the gospel, we will become more like our Savior, and we will want to be forever bound to family members.

The divine, transforming influence of the Christmas season is tangible and powerful. If necessary, we can choose to allow it to mend broken family relationships. In the beloved tale *A Christmas Carol*, Charles Dickens writes of the magical power of the season that inspires mankind to loftier thoughts and pursuits. Scrooge's nephew Fred explains, "I have always thought of Christmas time as a good time: a kind, forgiving, charitable, pleasant time: the only time I know of, in the long calendar of the year, when men and women seem by one consent to open their shut-up hearts freely. . . ."[1]

The holiday, or better said, "the Holy Day," of Christmas has the power to alter us in unexpected ways. It focuses our thoughts on Christ, on repentance and forgiveness, on family and relationships, and on all that truly matters in life. Dickens describes the miraculous conversion of Scrooge's Christmas experience, noting that

> Some people laughed to see the alteration in [Ebeneezer Scrooge], but he let them laugh, and little heeded them; for he was wise enough to know that nothing ever happened on this globe, for good, at which some people did not have their fill of laughter in the outset; and knowing that such as these would be blind any way, he thought it quite as well that they should wrinkle up their eyes in grins, as have the malady in less attractive form. His own heart laughed: and that was quite enough for him.[2]

Wise holiday observers know that the Christmas season can work a magical transformation in the hearts of all who embrace it because the enchantment of the season softens our hearts and beckons us to Christ.

The Christmas season can also magically alter our perception of the simple objects that surround us. If we choose to seek Christ, then even very simple objects of Christmas can transform into powerful symbols of Him, of brotherly love, of kindness. American author Washington Irving observed the magical power of the Christmas season:

> There is something in the very season of the year that gives a charm to the festivity of Christmas . . . Our thoughts are more concentrated; our friendly sympathies more aroused. We feel more sensibly the charm of each other's society, and are brought more closely together by dependence on each other for enjoyment. Heart calleth to heart and we draw pleasures from the deep wells of living kindness."[3]

Clearly, the unusual, divine transforming power of the season that turns our thoughts to Christ and our hope for eternal life can only be explained as the enabling power of the Atonement.

A wise Christian states, "Let us not spend Christmas . . . but let us keep Christmas in our hearts and in our lives."[4] As we choose to allow the season to change us for the better, we will yearn throughout the year for the Christmas season to transform us into true disciples.

"I will honor Christmas in my heart, and try to keep it all the year."

– Charles Dickens

1 Charles Dickens, *A Christmas Carol*, London: Bradbury and Evans, Printers, Whitefriars (1843), 8–9.

2 Ibid., 165.

3 Richard Henry Stoddard, *The Works of Washington Irving*, Pollard & Moss (1882), 48.

4 Peter Marshall, 80th Congress, 1st session, *Congressional Record* 19 Dec. 1947, pt. 9:11673.

The words of this anonymous essay artfully describe how the Christmas season's mystical power to bring us to Christ actually happens:

> I am the Christmas Spirit. I enter the home of poverty and cause pale-faced children to open wide their eyes in pleased wonder. I cause the miser to release his clutched hand, thus painting a bright spot upon his soul.
>
> I cause the aged to remember their youth and to laugh in the glad old way. I bring romance to child-hood and brighten dreams woven with magic.
>
> I cause eager feet to climb dark stairways with filled baskets, leaving behind hearts amazed at the good-ness of the world.
>
> I cause the prodigal to pause in his wild and wasteful way and send to anxious love some little token, which releases glad tears, washing away the hard lines of sorrow.
>
> I enter dark prison cells, causing scarred manhood to remember what might have been and pointing to better days yet to come.
>
> I enter the still white home of pain, and there lips that are too weak to speak just tremble in silent, eloquent gratitude.
>
> In a thousand ways I cause this weary old world to look up into the face of God and for a few moments forget everything that is small and wretched. *You see, I am the Christmas Spirit.*[5]

Certainly, the Christmas Spirit is the Spirit of Christ. It infuses the season with the transforming and enabling power to change us. The season inspires us to cheerfully seek Christ. It illuminates the spiritual essence of all mankind and the binding ties of the human family. And it leads the wise to Christ.

WHAT IS THE HISTORY OF THE CHRISTMAS SEASON?

The word *Christmas* derives from Old English *Christes maesse* or the Middle English *Christenmasse*. In the congregational Christian context, *Christmas* refers to Communion or Sacrament, the act of honoring Jesus Christ by remembering His atoning sacrifice of body

---

5 Thomas S. Monson, Christmas Devotional, 2011.

"[Christmas] comes every year and will go on forever. And along with Christmas belong the keepsakes and the customs. Those humble, everyday things a mother clings to, and ponders, like Mary in the secret spaces of her heart."

– Marjorie Holmes

and blood. At Christmastime, remembering both the birth and life of the Lord is seeking spiritual union with Him, honoring and worshiping Him, and finding emotional closeness to Him.

In pre-Christian times, most cultures from the northern hemisphere conducted late December festivals to celebrate the end of short winter days and the return of longer days of summer. At the time of winter solstice, many celebrations welcomed the lengthening of daylight hours with unruly parties and overall wickedness.[6] These celebrations commemorated the "unconquered Sun," signifying the lengthening of days after December 21.

Early Christians disliked the heathen celebration, and so they chose their own celebration for greater light after the winter solstice by celebrating the birth of God's unconquered Son. Saint Augustine explained, "We hold this day holy, not like the pagans because of the birth of the sun, but because of Him who made it." Christmas thus replaced the wild and worldly winter solstice celebrations such as Saturnalia, Mithras, Kalends, and other pre-Christian festivities, all of which celebrated the rebirth of the sun or Sol Invictus.[7] Clearly, the very origin of the Christmas season itself bears record of Jesus Christ.

---

6 One such celebration was that of Saturnalia, a Roman festival from December 17 to 24. The festival was intended to commemorate the beginning of longer days following the winter solstice. Accordingly, part of the celebration included an untying of ropes to free Saturn, the Roman god of agriculture, at his temple. It was an important festival, involving sacrifices, slave and master role reversal, gambling, gift-giving, and wild celebrations and debauchery. In essence, it was a time to eat, drink, and be merry. The replacement of such celebrations with Christmas commenced the celebration of a season in which faithful followers could draw closer to Heavenly Father and His Son.

7 Winter solstice festivities commemorated the sun gods. These winter celebrations arose out of the observation of the yearly cycles of winter (death) and spring (resurrection). It is the authors' belief that these early observations and practices to commemorate a time of rejuvenation each spring reflect an imperfect or undeveloped understanding of the prophesied advent of the only true and living Son of God, Jesus Christ. In this regard, even nature and legends attempting to explain the cycle of nature testify of the mission of the Savior, who

WHAT WE DO TO FIND TESTIMONIES OF CHRIST IN THE CHRISTMAS SEASON

Each year, several months before the Christmas season, at carefully spaced intervals, we begin to send short notes, texts, e-mails, or voice messages to our children: "Christmas is coming," or "Only __ days until Christmas," or "Emergency news: Christmas will soon be here!" The very mention of the season reminds our family to begin to include remembrance and worship of our Savior in all plans for our upcoming celebrations. Collectively, we plan for family worship, recreation, service projects, and new ways to seek Christ in Christmas.

WHAT YOU CAN DO TO FIND TESTIMONIES OF CHRIST IN THE CHRISTMAS SEASON

We invite you to discover even more ways to seek Christ in your Christmas celebration this year. Here are some simple ideas that can enrich your Christmas season with testimonies of Christ. These easy traditions may help you continue to seek Christ as you plan your celebration.

We promise that rich blessings of peace, joy, and love will rest upon you and your loved ones as you diligently seek Christ in Christmas this year and always. Creating and preserving happy memories will help your family reflect upon and teach one another about Christ for many years to come.

---

came to earth bringing new life and light. The fact that prior legends reflect or imitate later actual events surrounding the birth and life of Jesus demonstrates the power of revelation to prophesy concerning the verity of Christ's coming. For example, Isaiah accurately foretold events in Jesus's life more than seven hundred years before Christ's birth (see Isaiah 53).

- Set aside a particular day for a traditional beginning of the Christmas season. Make this special day an invitation to your family members and friends to truly welcome Christ into all of their holiday customs. Serve a special festive treat. We suggest traditional homemade cinnamon rolls slathered with creamy red or green frosting and a glass of cold milk.

- Watch the movie, *The Nativity*. After the short five-minute film, invite each family member to share a favorite Christmas memory and how it testifies of Christ. Invite family members to commit to do their best to seek the true spirit of Christ throughout the season in every Christmas custom and tradition.

- Create a family Christmas hashtag such as #laycockfamchristmas where family members can share testimonies of Christ through text and photos and compile them in an organized manner.

- Create a shared family Dropbox folder (or something similar) to collect family Christmas photos and memories of Christ-centered family activities. Use these photos to create an inexpensive photo book using Shutterfly or another online program so that you will always remember the ways your family comes closer to Christ during the holiday season.

- To eliminate stress, create a Google, Cozi App, SquareHub App, or other family calendar of family activities.

- Make your own Christmas potpourri. Pleasant Christmas aromas can be powerful ties to happy memories and thoughts of the Savior. We love the wonderful smell of Christmas potpourri wafting through our home during the Christmas season. This recipe is a family favorite.

Christmas Season Scents

INGREDIENTS

> Orange peels
>
> Sliced apples and/or apple cores
>
> Cinnamon stick
>
> 1 tsp. vanilla
>
> 1 tsp. cinnamon
>
> 5–6 whole cloves

DIRECTIONS

> Put all ingredients in a saucepan. Cover with water. Bring to a boil then reduce to a simmer. Continue to let your mixture simmer, and it will create a wonderful Christmas aroma. Remember to watch your pan so that it doesn't boil out of water and burn. You can use each batch for a few weeks. We drain the water off after each use. Then we like to leave it in the pan on the stove so that it's ready to use again.

Delicious and Easy Christmas Cinnamon Rolls

INGREDIENTS

1 cup (2 sticks) margarine or butter

1 cup sugar

1 cup boiling water

2 packages active dry yeast

1 cup warm water

1 egg

5–7 cups all-purpose flour

½ cup (1 stick) margarine or butter, melted and divided

⅓ cup brown sugar, packed and divided

Cinnamon to taste

⅓ cup red- and/or green-colored sugar (optional)

Cream cheese frosting, colored red and/or green

INSTRUCTIONS

In a large bowl, blend together 2 sticks butter, sugar, and boiling water. Dissolve yeast in warm water; add egg and whisk with fork; stir into butter mixture. Add flour, a little at a time, until dough cleans the sides of the bowl. Cover bowl with towel, and let rise until double. Roll out half of the dough to a 12" x 8" rectangle; spread with ½ stick melted margarine or butter. Sprinkle with half the brown sugar and cinnamon. You could also sprinkle colored sugar sprinkles to add festivity. Beginning with the long end, roll up, jelly roll style, and cut with serrated knife or dental floss into 12 slices. Repeat with the remaining half of dough. Place on greased cookie sheet, leaving about one inch between each roll. Cover with towel, and let double in size. Bake at 350 degrees for 15–20 minutes. When cool, frost. Makes 2 dozen.

CHAPTER 2

SANTA CLAUS

HOW DOES SANTA CLAUS CONFIRM OUR TESTIMONY OF CHRIST?

Santa Claus is a popular part of Christmas celebrations. For many, he has become a magical symbol of magnanimous giving. As a symbol of Christlike behavior, Santa represents what is good in mankind. His encouragement to obey and do good combined with his excitement to share kindness can turn even the most dismal of winter days into a celebration of happiness and love. In fact, when viewed through spiritual eyes, the beloved jolly red elf inspires us and helps us to see the Savior's example of anonymous service, undaunted love, and selfless giving. Santa's reputation for selflessness and generosity also exemplifies and encourages us to put into practice Christ's teachings to be full of charity and to show love toward all men. Christ says: "For I was an hungered, and ye gave me meat: I was thirsty, and ye gave me drink: I was a stranger, and ye took me in: Naked, and ye clothed me: I was sick, and ye visited me: I was in prison, and ye came unto me . . . . Verily I say unto you, Inasmuch as ye have done it unto one of the least of these my brethren, ye have done it unto me" (Matthew 25:35–40). Thus, the traditions of "playing Santa," "subbing for Santa," or becoming a "Santa's helper" all lead us to emulate Christ's example of noble and altruistic service and giving. President James E. Faust wisely said:

No one can measure the effect of an unselfish act of kindness. By small, simple things great things do indeed come to pass. Of course, gifts given and gifts received make Christmas special. For many children, Christmas Eve is a very long night as they look forward with eager anticipation to the gifts Santa brings, which is why children love Santa Claus.[8]

An anonymous author describes Santa Claus this way:

First of all, he's a joyous individual. . . . Next, Santa Claus is interested in making others happy. He increases the happy moments in the life of everyone he meets. He loves his work; he gets fun out of his job. He is childlike, simple, humble, sincere, and forgiving. Finally, he is a giver. His philosophy is to give himself away in service. He is a friend to everyone. He smiles. Perhaps you and I could attain greater happiness if we emulated Santa Claus a little more, for his way is the way of the Infant Jesus.

---

8 James E. Faust, "The Man Who Would Be Santa," First Presidency Christmas Devotional, December 6, 1998.

"Jolly old St. Nicholas,
Lean your ear this way!
Don't you tell a single soul
What I'm going to say;
Christmas Eve is coming soon;
Now, you dear old man,
Whisper what you'll bring to me:
Tell me if you can.
When the clock is striking twelve,
When I'm fast asleep,
Down the chimney broad and black,
With your pack you'll creep.
All the stockings you will find
Hanging in a row;
Mine will be the shortest one,
You'll be sure to know.
Johnny wants a pair of skates,
Susie wants a sled,
Nellie wants a picture book,
yellow, blue and red.
Now I think I'll leave to you
what to give the rest.
Choose for me dear Santa Claus;
You will know what's best."

When we consider that the word *Santa* means "saint" or "sacred," we see that even his name causes us to think of sacred things.

Santa brings with him an opportunity to create memories of love, togetherness, and kindness. Remember, the greatest act of sincere service was offered when Christ began the journey toward completing the Atonement in Gethsemane and on the cross of Calvary. While others slept, Christ toiled to perform the infinite Atonement, and we are recipients of that gift anew whenever we repent, make covenants, and experience the healing influence of Christ's Atonement.

Although there are those who claim that Santa draws our attention away from the real purpose for celebrating Christmas, the Apostle Paul explains that the pure can find goodness in all things: "Unto the pure all things are pure: but unto them that are defiled and unbelieving is nothing pure; but even their mind and conscience is defiled" (Titus 1:15). As we practice the Santa tradition, let us think of it and speak of it as an opportunity to put into practice the examples of giving that Christ has shown us. Santa Claus becomes an example of a faithful follower of Christ because he demonstrates godly love.

Even Santa's clothing can remind the wise to think of Jesus Christ. The crimson color of his magical suit reminds us of the blood that Christ freely spilt for us. The beautiful white trim conjures images of purity and cleanliness associated with the Son of God. Santa often uses a staff in the shape of a shepherd's crook, reminding us of the good shepherd that Jesus symbolizes.

Throughout His mortal ministry, Christ admonished those whom He blessed to "tell no man" (see Matthew 8:4, 16:20, 17:9; Mark 7:36, 8:30, 9:9; Luke 5:14, 8:56, and 9:21). He sought to freely bless lives through His teaching, example of kindness—especially to children—and His miraculous healings until the last days of His earthly ministry. He sought no recompense. And despite the many miracles He performed, Christ's greatest gifts to mankind are those of the infinite Atonement and the triumphal Resurrection: "Greater love hath no man than this, that a man lay down his life for his friends" (John 15:13). As we practice the Santa tradition, we can remember the example of a fellow follower of Christ and share in that same anonymous giving and loving kindness.

WHAT IS THE HISTORY OF THE LEGEND OF SANTA CLAUS?

Origins of the Santa Claus tradition vary. In fact, even his name varies, including names such as Father Christmas, Sinterklaas, Kris Kringle, and Saint Nicholas. Some people even contend that Santa, or Saint Nicholas, was not real. Nothing could be farther from the truth. According to historical accounts, Saint Nicholas served as a faithful bishop, typifying love and compassion for children as well as anonymous service to the poor and needy.

According to both history and legend, Saint Nicholas was a real person and a prisoner for Christ. He served as the bishop of Myra. According to ancient biographers, he was born into a wealthy family in the city of Patara around AD 270. Nicholas's parents raised him to be a righteous Christian. Following the untimely death of his parents due to an epidemic,

young Nicholas dedicated his life and his inherited wealth to helping the poor and needy. Known for his generosity, his kind heart is reflected in many legends of anonymous giving and consistent charity.

Historians and legend also relate that Nicholas even saved the lives of children in peril. Nicholas helped to lead his congregation through one of the most difficult times in Christian history. In approximately AD 303, the Roman emperor ordered brutal and vicious persecution of all Christians, forcing them to make sacrifices to pagan gods. Nicholas and his faithful followers refused. Romans imprisoned the noncompliant Christians, including Nicholas, and exposed them to torture, feeding them to wild animals and forcing them to fight gladiators. Those who survived the persecution came to be called Saints. Thus, upon emerging from prison, Bishop Nicholas became Saint Nicholas. He faithfully served his congregation for an additional thirty years.

In 1881, US illustrator Thomas Nast, a cartoonist and caricaturist considered to be the "Father of the American Cartoon," created an illustration of Santa Claus. That illustration, complete with a wreath upon Santa's head and an arm full of toys, has become the modern depiction of Santa. An author named Clement Clarke Moore also helped to define the image of our modern-day Santa in his immortal poem, "A Visit from St. Nicholas," also known as "'Twas the Night Before Christmas." The well-known poem was first published anonymously in the *Troy Sentinel* in New York on December 23, 1823. This poem created an image of Santa Claus—including his attire, his physical appearance, the timing for his visit, his sleigh, his gift-giving tradition, and even the number and names of his reindeer. Based on legends, illustrations, and poetry, children around the world easily recognize Santa as a giver of good gifts to obedient children on the night of Christ's birth.

Continuing the happy tradition of including Santa in Christmas celebrations, Francis P. Church wrote a famous editorial response to eight-year-old Virginia O'Hanlon's question, "Is there a Santa Claus?" In his famous confirmatory response, Church declares:

> "*Yes, Virginia, there is a Santa Claus.* He exists as certainly as love and generosity and devotion exist, and you know that they abound and give to your life its highest beauty and joy. Alas! How dreary would be the world if there were no Santa Claus! It would be as dreary as if there were no Virginias. There would be no child-like faith then, no poetry, no romance to make tolerable this existence. We should have no enjoyment, except in sense and sight. The eternal light with which childhood fills the world would be extinguished."

We join Mr. Church in confirming that Santa Claus exists wherever there is an unselfish desire to help the poor, give anonymously to the needy, share love with the forsaken, or bring delight and joy to children. That we may all honor Christmas as Santa does is our wish this Christmas and always.

WHAT WE HAVE DONE TO FIND TESTIMONIES OF CHRIST IN THE LEGEND OF SANTA CLAUS

One year, we learned of a young family in need. The children of this family were about the same ages as our children, and we wanted to help make their Christmas merry. The parents

were struggling students at a nearby university, and we knew they felt lonely, as they were unable to travel home to visit their extended families for the holidays. We also knew they had no extra money to spend on Christmas that year, so we prayed for guidance to know how we could help. We knew we didn't have enough money to do it all on our own, so we invited two other families to our home to plan a "Secret Santa" for the sweet little family.

Our children scurried about like little elves during the next few weeks as we gathered and prepared Christmas for our friends. We made assignments for everyone to provide certain parts of the Christmas surprise that we would all deliver. On Christmas Eve, we dressed warmly, took our flashlights and field glasses, and set out to deliver Christmas.

We explained to our children that we were Santa's helpers and that the word *Santa* means "saint," which is what we all strive to be (see Ephesians 2:18–20). Our group watched through binoculars as the three dads placed our surprise on the family's front doorstep, knocked loudly, shook some Santa bells, and ran like the wind so as not to be discovered. We had so much fun that we decided to make it a yearly tradition. We now call this our yearly "Christmas Caper."

WHAT YOU CAN DO TO FIND TESTIMONIES OF CHRIST IN THE LEGEND OF SANTA CLAUS

- Gather your family together on a special evening in early November and plan a secret, anonymous visit from your family to someone in need. Invite each family member to come to the gathering prepared with ideas of whom you should secretly serve that year. Be sure to make the selection process a prayerful and sweet event. We continue to work on our secret plans during the months of November and December, assuring that we are ready to carry out the secret delivery of our Christmas Caper on Christmas Eve. The planning is truly joyous, but delivering is always the most memorable aspect of our Christmas Caper! Without a doubt, our past Christmas Capers are the most frequently and lovingly reviewed memories when our family gathers to celebrate Christmas. Remember that repetition is an excellent teacher, so each year when you gather for the planning phase of your Christmas Caper, remind everyone that *Santa* means "saint" or "sacred" and that each person in your family is a saintly Santa helper.

- Read "'Twas the Night Before Christmas" as a family. Discuss ways Santa serves others like Christ does. Commit to become Santas or Saints that provide anonymous service and gifts of love that remind everyone of the most important, selfless gift of the Atonement of Jesus Christ not only during the Christmas season but also throughout the entire year.

- Prepare Rice Krispie treats in the shape of Santa hats. They are fun and easy to make. The entire family will want to help. Make them and eat them together, discussing ways you can emulate the anonymous, selfless giving of Saint Nicholas and, in similitude, Jesus.

Kris Kringle Krispie Treats

INGREDIENTS

3 Tablespoons butter or margarine

1 10-oz. package regular marshmallows or 4 cups miniature marshmallows

Red food coloring

6 cups Rice Krispies, divided

Red sugar decorating sprinkles

DIRECTIONS

Melt butter in a large saucepan over low heat. Add marshmallows and stir until completely melted. Remove from heat. Divide the mixture so you can add red food coloring to ⅔ and leave the other ⅓ white.

Add 4 cups Rice Krispies to larger mixture and 2 cups to the smaller. Stir until coated with marshmallow mixture.

Shape the red mixture into Santa hats (triangles) and place on wax paper. Sprinkle triangles with red sugar decorating sprinkles. Gently push on the sprinkles to make them stick to the Rice Krispies hats. Press a small ball of white mixture on top of each triangle and line the bottom of each with white mixture.

Our children LOVE to help make these. Don't be overly concerned with how they look. It's more important for everyone to enjoy the journey! Eat and enjoy!

CHAPTER 3

CHRISTMAS STOCKINGS

HOW DOES THE CHRISTMAS STOCKING CONFIRM OUR TESTIMONY OF CHRIST?

Each Christmas season, many who celebrate the birth of Christ practice the custom of hanging stockings near the chimney, carefully suspending them from the mantle above the fireplace. They can be fashioned of anything from humble, homespun yarn to elaborate fabrics trimmed with velvet, fur, and sparkling jewels. Regardless of the type of stocking, this Christmas custom is accompanied by the expectation that Santa will arrive while we sleep and fill our Christmas stocking with gifts and sweets and surprises of all kinds.

As we ponder this fun tradition, we can find a poignant testimony of our Savior in it. Just as Santa fills the Christmas stockings of those who have been good, our loving Savior fills our lives with treasures of kindness, charity, and love when we are obedient to God's commandments. The Christmas stocking, brimming with bountiful offerings, reminds us of the power of Jesus Christ and His restored gospel to fill each of us with joy, unselfishness, and fulfillment. Our Savior fills our lives with all that truly matters.

For as long as you can remember, you have probably believed that by hanging your stocking on Christmas Eve, you would be rewarded—that magically, before Christmas morning, Santa would fill your stocking with gifts and goodies galore. After all, it would not be Christmas without our cherished stocking tradition; however, it is quite unfortunate that most participants do not know of the story that inspires the tradition. In its origin, you will find meaning and richness in this tradition that clearly bears record of Jesus the Christ and His earthly mission.

WHAT IS THE HISTORY OF THE CHRISTMAS STOCKING?

The legend of the Christmas stocking takes us back in time to when Saint Nicholas was serving as bishop of Myra. Among those in his congregation was a poor family consisting of a destitute widower and his three daughters. The poor father could barely provide food and lodging for his family, so it was clearly out of the question for him to be able to provide a marriage dowry for any one of his three daughters. A dowry consisted of the goods or estate that a young woman could bring to the family of her future husband in marriage and usually consisted of land, precious metals, or both. Without a dowry, a young woman's prospects for a good marriage were reduced, in most cases, to zero. Knowing of these circumstances, St. Nicholas determined to bless the lives of the suffering family by anonymously giving a gift that would not only be meaningful but also serve the young women's families over a lifetime.

Knowing that each night the poor girls must hang their only pair of freshly washed

"'Twas the night before Christmas, When all through the house Not a creature was stirring, Not even a mouse; The stockings all hung by the chimney with care, In hopes that Saint Nicholas soon would be there."

– Clement Moore

stockings near the fire to dry them for use the next morning, Saint Nicholas secretly crept into the humble home one night and left gold coins in the eldest daughter's stocking. His wise and generous gift provided her much-needed dowry. When the family awoke the next morning, the young woman was astonished to discover the golden gift in her shabby stocking. Saint Nicholas secretly repeated his generous gift for each of the other two daughters.

Despite the bishop's desire to remain anonymous, the girls' father discovered Saint Nicholas as he placed coins in the youngest daughter's stocking. Bishop Nicholas pleaded with the poor father to keep the gift—and the secret. But the father was unable to contain his delight and gratitude for the generous gifts, and he broke his promise of confidentiality. He shared the story of his benefactor's kindness and generosity with all who would listen.

From this example of selfless, anonymous giving, the tradition of the Christmas stocking was born. Just as Saint Nicholas's gifts filled this family's desperate situation with the brightness of hope and love, so our Savior fills our desperate longing for salvation and eternal life with the precious gift of His Atonement.

WHAT WE HAVE DONE TO FIND TESTIMONIES OF CHRIST IN THE CHRISTMAS STOCKING

One Christmas, we helped our daughter plan a gift for a friend whose family had suffered some financial setbacks. A few days before Christmas, our daughter was able to enter into her friend's house without anyone knowing. While there, she hid a gift inside the Christmas stocking of her friend without being discovered. We discussed the story of Saint Nicholas following the example of Christ and giving meaningful gifts to those in need. Our daughter savors the memory created by that act of kindness, and now, more than a decade later, her service continues to bring feelings of love and kindness. As our daughter experienced her friend's delight with having received the gift, our daughter's joy multiplied, and she sparkles with happiness whenever she speaks of it.

WHAT YOU CAN DO TO FIND TESTIMONIES OF CHRIST IN THE CHRISTMAS STOCKING

- Each year, have your children open the gifts in their Christmas stockings while you remind them of how the Christmas stocking bears record of Christ.

- Place a gift unique to each child in his or her Christmas stocking that will be realized sometime in the coming year—anything from a voucher for a planned activity to a more

elaborate gift like a coupon for a family vacation. Ensure that these gifts carry your love and desire for family unity. Explain how gifts of self remind us of the gift of Christ's Atonement.

- As you hang the family Christmas stockings, recount the story of how they became an important tradition. Help your family or friends understand that this custom bears record of Christ in the important lesson that it teaches to give meaningful gifts to those in need, as Jesus did.

- Help your family members to make a plan to place a secret, meaningful gift in the Christmas stocking of a friend, family member, or loved one.

- Buy a bag of chocolate coins wrapped in gold foil paper to share with family members as you discuss how wonderful it is to give and receive anonymous gifts of love and kindness.

- Read the book *Christmas Oranges* by Linda Bethers. Discuss how important small gifts of love and kindness are. Remind family members how gifts of kindness remind us of Christ. Enjoy dipping oranges in chocolate and eating the treat as you read and talk.

Christmas Oranges

INGREDIENTS

    5–6 oranges or clementines, peeled and separated in pieces (make sure they are dry)

    Chocolate chips, almond bark, or Hershey's chocolate bars for dipping

DIRECTIONS

    Melt chocolate in microwave-safe bowl. Dip oranges in chocolate, and place on a plate or dish in the refrigerator for 10 minutes. Remove from refrigerator when ready to serve.

CHAPTER 4

CHRISTMAS TREE

HOW DOES THE CHRISTMAS TREE CONFIRM OUR TESTIMONY OF CHRIST?

The custom of placing a Christmas tree in our homes each year bears record of Jesus Christ's triumph over death and gives us a living example of an object capable of overcoming the long, cold months of winter. The evergreen tree symbolizes everlasting and eternal life because it maintains its vibrant color and existence, even while other trees die in the cycle of seasons. The evergreen, through its straight growth toward the sun, symbolizes the way in which Jesus guides us toward light and how He is the way, the truth, and the life (see John 14:6). The triangular shape of the Christmas tree demonstrates Christ's role as a member of the Godhead and His place on the right hand of God the Father.

Christ's Triumph over Death

The Christmas evergreen, with its ability to triumph over the death of winter, testifies of everlasting life and the glorious Resurrection of our Lord. The evergreen tree reminds us of the new life and hope that entered the world on the night of our Savior's birth. It is the hope for new life that Christ offers. The tree offers even deeper significance when seen in the context of Christ's explanation that He is the true vine and His disciples are the branches (see John 15:1–17). In this beautiful imagery, we recognize that, as disciples of Christ, we, the branches, are wholly dependent on Christ, the vine from which all life flows. Christ explains: "I am the vine, ye are the branches: He that abideth in me, and I in him, the same bringeth forth much fruit: for without me ye can do nothing" (John 15:5).

The ever-living nature of the Christmas tree reminds us that Jesus is risen from the dead and will return to the earth as promised. As we abide in Him—the true vine—we have life and are able to become fruitful. Jesus explained that a good tree brings forth good fruit; thus, "by their fruits, ye shall know them" (see Matthew 7:18–20). At His glorious Second Coming, every knee shall bow and every tongue confess that He is God's own Son, the Redeemer of all the world (see Romans 14:11).

Christ Is the Way, the Truth, and the Life

The fact that evergreen trees grow "true" or straight heavenward, always seeking the light, teaches us to live as Jesus did. Throughout His life, Jesus always did the will of His

"*And out of the ground made the Lord God to grow every tree that is pleasant to the sight, and good for food; the tree of life also in the midst of the garden, and the tree of knowledge of good and evil.*"

—*Genesis 2:9*

Father in Heaven. "Then answered Jesus and said unto them, Verily, verily, I say unto you, The Son can do nothing of himself, but what he seeth the Father do: for what things soever he doeth, these also doeth the Son likewise" (John 5:19). Christ's life becomes the example of perfection introduced in the Sermon on the Mount: "Be ye therefore perfect, even as your Father which is in heaven is perfect" (Matthew 5:48). Christ shows us the perfect example of how to increase "in wisdom and stature, and in favour with God and man" (Luke 2:52). The Christmas tree can teach us to seek light and grow straight and true in the gospel of Christ.

Christ's Role as a Member of the Godhead

The three-point triangular shape of a Christmas tree serves as a reminder of the place Jesus occupies in the Holy Trinity at the right hand of our Heavenly Father. In the tree, we find an image of the doctrinal statement that God, Jesus Christ, and the Holy Ghost form the Godhead as three individual beings united by one purpose.

Christ Brings Hope of Life Everlasting

The Christmas tree stands as a symbol of the tree of life. In turn, the tree of life represents the love of God. "For God so loved the world, that he gave his only begotten Son, that whosoever believeth in him should not perish, but have everlasting life" (John 3:16). Just as the tree of life represents the eternal love of God, the Christmas tree can remind us of the love God offers us through the atoning sacrifice of His Son. The knowledge that we can be partakers of salvation and exaltation is the ultimate source of hope. Following Christ through repentance, baptism, and continued faithfulness will enable us to become the "first fruits" of Jesus, among those caught up to Him at the time of the Second Coming.

WHAT IS THE HISTORY OF THE CHRISTMAS TREE?

Many beautiful legends explain the origin of the time-honored tradition of bringing evergreen trees into our homes at Christmas. For example, in the eighth century, a well-known English monk by the name of Boniface devoted his life to the service of God and served numerous missions to spread the gospel. According to legend, Boniface came upon a group of men gathered around an oak tree. The misguided men were in the process of sacrificing a young boy to the mythological god of thunder. In outrage, Boniface struck the oak tree where the men stood. The great oak fell to the ground, and in its place appeared a delicate evergreen. Boniface pointed to the tree as a sign and testimony of Jesus Christ. He described the triangular shape as a symbol of the Holy Trinity. In the presence of the evergreen tree, the boy was saved and the men repented, vowing faithfulness to Jesus.

As a result of the telling and retelling of this legend, many people in Europe began to bring the sacred evergreen into their homes as a sign of their belief in Christianity. Many times, these early Christians suspended the trees from the ceiling in an upside-down position, likely so that the pinnacle of the tree, which represents God the Father, would be closest to them. This legend strengthens and gives meaning to our own Christmas tree tradition as a symbol of our allegiance to God the Father, Jesus Christ, and the Holy Ghost and our never-ending desire to be closer to our Heavenly Father.

Among the most cherished legends of the Christmas tree is the experience of Martin Luther, one of the initiators of the Protestant Reformation. The story is told of Luther's wintery night's journey through a snow-frosted forest of evergreens. Pausing to rest, Luther peered at the starlight sifting through the snow-laden branches of the pine trees. The beauty of the starlight glistening on the frosty branches caught the man's imagination, so he cut down an evergreen and took it into his home to show his family the extraordinary sight. He attached candles to the branches of the tree to recreate the effect of the starlight, and the lighted-Christmas-tree tradition was born.

A royal family in England also helped mainstream the Christmas tree in our present-day celebrations. German-born Prince Albert, husband of Queen Victoria, brought festive Christmas traditions with him from Germany. Among these

traditions, Prince Albert introduced the practice of decorating a Christmas tree to Windsor Palace. In 1846, the popular Prince Albert and his wife were pictured in the *Illustrated London News* along with their decorated family Christmas tree. Because of the couple's tremendous popularity, the tradition of decorating a Christmas tree immediately became stylish. In an effort to emulate the practices of the popular queen and prince, British citizens began decorating their own Christmas trees, and the practice eventually spread to America and beyond.

WHAT WE HAVE DONE TO FIND TESTIMONIES OF CHRIST IN THE CHRISTMAS TREE

I (Larry) remember how a simple little Christmas tree changed my perspective of Christmas. I attended a children's Sunday School activity where the teachers invited each age group to help provide a Christmas surprise for an elderly couple living in our neighborhood. Some classes donated Christmas goodies and canned foods gathered in a bushel basket. Others brought simple decorations. I donated a small Christmas tree that my mother had helped me cut from the top of our own family Christmas tree, which was too tall to fit in our home. Another child donated a small strand of lights. We all stood on the porch of the elderly couple's home and sang Christmas carols until the little old woman opened the door. The crowd of children pushed me forward into the small room. I held the tiny tree in one hand and the bushel basket's wire handle in the other. The home felt cold and uninviting with no trace of Christmas anywhere to be seen.

Magically, within seconds, the home transformed. The small tree and humble strand of lights brightened the tiny room. Glowing warmly, the colorful tree changed the surroundings from cold and lonely to warm and inviting. The small, hunched-over little couple began to cry. The old gentleman wiped away a tear and quietly said, "Look, Mama, they brought us Christmas."

Turning to leave, we began to sing "Silent Night." The memory of what a small Christmas tree did to bring the spirit of Christmas to a couple in need will forever remain in my heart and mind. As Laura Ingalls Wilder observed: "Our hearts grow tender with childhood memories and love of kindred, and we are better throughout the year for having, in spirit, become a child again at Christmastime."

WHAT YOU CAN DO TO FIND TESTIMONIES OF CHRIST IN THE CHRISTMAS TREE

- Plan a traditional day to select and decorate your Christmas tree. We usually decorate our tree on the Saturday following Thanksgiving. Set aside plenty of time to savor the event and to create happy memories for all involved. Think of the process as a memory-making activity and not merely a task to complete. Remember to recount the histories that relate to the various family decorations.

- Invite family members or friends to share favorite Christmas memories as you gather around the Christmas tree to visit and reminisce about past Christmases.

- Remember to take time during the busy Christmas season to frequently gather your loved ones in the tree's glowing presence and discuss how your Christmas tree bears record of Christ.

- Bake some delicious Christmas goodies as a family. Our favorite tree-trimming snack is Christmas-tree-shaped, hand-decorated sugar cookies with cold, frothy milk. We love to decorate the cookies as we talk about the many ways the Christmas tree helps us remember the Savior.

Christmas Tree Sugar Cookies

INGREDIENTS

    1 cup shortening

    2 cups sugar

    2 eggs

    1 cup sour cream

    1 teaspoon vanilla extract

    1 teaspoon almond extract

    1 teaspoon lemon extract

    4 teaspoons baking powder

    ½ teaspoon salt

    ¼ teaspoon ground nutmeg

    4½ cups flour

DIRECTIONS

Cream shortening and sugar. Add one egg at a time. Stir in sour cream and extracts. Add dry ingredients (blended/sifted). Refrigerate dough for 30 minutes, then roll out and cut with cookie cutters.

Bake at 350 degrees for 15–18 minutes.

FROSTING

    8 ounces cream cheese

    ½ cup butter, softened

    2 teaspoon vanilla extract

    1 pound powdered sugar

    Green food coloring

While cookies cool, cream the cream cheese and butter. After creamed, blend in vanilla and powdered sugar until smooth. Add green food coloring.

Be sure to have an assortment of fun, colorful candies to decorate your trees. Your family will have a delightful time as you create beautiful Christmas tree cookies and remember the symbolism of the Christmas tree.

CHAPTER 5

CHRISTMAS TREE ORNAMENTS

HOW DO CHRISTMAS TREE ORNAMENTS CONFIRM OUR TESTIMONY OF CHRIST?

The tradition of decorating the Christmas tree with bright ornaments bears record of Christ by reminding us that through obedience we all may partake of the fruit of God's love found on the tree of life (see Genesis 3:22; see also Revelation 2:7). In many homes, ornaments are carefully selected and carry important memories of special events like the birth of a child, a special vacation, or any other happy memory. Families adorn their tree's branches with beautiful memories as much as with the bright ornaments. The warm radiance of a decorated Christmas tree is an essential element of holiday celebration, but more importantly, a decorated Christmas tree adds another reminder of Jesus Christ and God's love.

Treasured family Christmas tree ornaments present symbols of Christian faith. If we choose to consider the context of their deeper meaning, our ornaments become a representation of the fruit of the tree of life. As we enjoy the beauty of our modern-day tree ornaments, we may also choose to ponder how the sweet, enjoyable fruit of the tree of life helps us feel joy.

Each year as we place ornaments on our Christmas trees, we may choose to remember that we all are invited to partake of the fruit of the tree of life through faith, repentance, baptism, the gift of the Holy Ghost, and enduring to the end. Christmas tree ornaments present colorful and vibrant images of the love of God. They prompt us to think of God's greatest gift to mankind, even the gift of eternal life available to all who partake.

WHAT IS THE HISTORY OF CHRISTMAS TREE ORNAMENTS?

During the Middle Ages, early Christians sought tangible, physical means to teach religious values and share gospel stories. For example, many times the unlearned or illiterate Christians had their first introduction to Bible stories by looking at the artfully designed depictions of such stories in the stained-glass windows of medieval churches and cathedrals. Among other means used to teach Bible stories, believers conducted morality plays, or biblical dramatic presentations of Bible stories, beginning with the story of Adam and Eve. Central to the history of the Garden of Eden is the tree of knowledge of good and evil, and even more important to our eternal destiny is the tree of life.

Anciently, in the presentation of the Creation and the Garden of Eden, an evergreen tree decorated with fruit represented the tree of life. The evergreen tree was used for its vibrant green color, showing the hope of new life even in the dead of winter. Early Christians attached fruit to the trees to create the effect of a living tree that was capable of bearing fruit. The fruit placed on the morality-play evergreens may very well have been the first Christmas tree ornaments.

"The ornaments upon our tree that glow all through the night
Remind us of the fruit of God placed on the tree of life.
The ornaments of Christmastime can teach of truth and light.
They symbolize God's precious love and help us choose the right.
The ornaments upon our tree will point us all to love.
They help us honor covenants that come from God above."

~Larry and Lisa Laycock

WHAT WE HAVE DONE TO FIND TESTIMONIES OF CHRIST IN CHRISTMAS TREE ORNAMENTS

When our children were young, we purchased a special red ornament box for each child. We made a tag for each box that was encased in plastic and decorated with Christmas images and the name of the child. They were thrilled to have a place to store their very own precious ornament gifts. Each year, we selected a distinct Christmas ornament for each child. We hid the ornaments in their Christmas stockings. They loved discovering their unique ornament every year. The children hung their ornaments on our tree each Christmas and reminisced about the year they received them until it came time for them to be married and start their own homes and Christmas traditions. It was a tender time when a child got married and received his or her ornament box, filled with fond memories and lovely ornaments. It is a satisfying experience to see the ornaments that now make their way into our grandchildren's Christmas stockings each year.

WHAT YOU CAN DO TO FIND TESTIMONIES OF CHRIST IN CHRISTMAS TREE ORNAMENTS

- We invite you to make it a family practice to search for and select a memory-making family ornament each year. The ornament could carry in itself an important meaning and then serve as a symbol of a special event like the birth of a child, a special vacation, or a fun memory.

- This activity could also be expanded to include starting individual ornament collections for your children or grandchildren by adding one simple, yet symbolic ornament each year. Symbolic ornaments could consist of representative pieces from a Nativity set. The ornaments could also reflect the symbols discussed in this book to help your children find and strengthen their testimonies of Christ during the celebration of Christmas.

- When we talk of how Christmas tree ornaments testify of Christ, we love to make caramel apples. We also enjoy other assorted fruits cut into bite-size pieces and dipped in yummy fruit dip. The snack reminds us of the fruit that grows on the tree of life as well as the fruits that were used anciently to decorate Christmas trees.

Christmas Apples

6 apples (green, gala, or red), washed and dried

1 14-ounce package of individually wrapped caramels, unwrapped

2 Tablespoon milk (or sweetened condensed milk)

6 craft sticks

DIRECTIONS

Remove the stems then wash and dry the apples. Press craft stick into top of apple.

Place parchment paper on a baking sheet.

Place the caramels in microwave-safe bowl with milk and heat for 2 minutes, stirring once. Allow to cool for a few seconds.

Dip and roll each apple in the melted caramel until covered then place on prepared baking sheet.

We like to dip apples in sugar/cinnamon, sprinkles, mini M&M's, or crushed candy bar pieces before letting them set.

Frosted Fruit Dip

INGREDIENTS

2 8-ounce packages cream cheese

½ cup Cool Whip

1 cup brown sugar

1 teaspoon vanilla extract

Fruit cut into bite-size pieces (apples, pears, oranges, strawberries, grapes, kiwi, etc.)

Blend all ingredients except fruit with hand mixer. Sometimes we like to add a few drops of food coloring to add a festive flare. Dip fruit and enjoy.

CHAPTER 6

ANGELS

HOW DO CHRISTMAS ANGELS CONFIRM OUR TESTIMONY OF CHRIST?

Our family's angel traditions have brought us great joy over the years. Each year, we look forward to placing the angels in our Nativity scenes because our angels always carry our thoughts to Christ. The tradition of decorating with Christmas angels bears record of Jesus Christ as we remember how angels foretold and celebrated Christ's first coming into the world. We use angels to top Christmas trees, to shape cookies, to decorate Christmas cards and letters, and to adorn our homes. Each angel at Christmastime reminds us of the many heavenly beings that heralded the birth of Christ (see Luke 2:13), including the appearance of the angel of the Lord to Mary (see Luke 1:26–31), an angel who appears in a dream to Joseph (Matthew 1:20), and the heavenly host of angels appearing to the shepherds (see Luke 2:13–14). It is comforting to consider that each scriptural angelic visit includes the words *fear not* (see Luke 1:13, 30; 2:10; Matthew 1:20). This angelic message of peace and comfort has not changed in more than two thousand years. Real Christmas angels find their origin in the scriptural accounts of the Nativity. Heavenly Father sent messengers to announce the birth of John the Baptist as well as the birth of Jesus Christ. The angel Gabriel, who dwells in the presence of God (see Luke 1:19), appeared to Zacharias, father of John the Baptist, telling him that God had granted him the blessing of a son who would go before the Savior "to make ready a people prepared for the Lord" (Luke 1:17).

The angel Gabriel was sent again from the presence of God into a city in Galilee, named Nazareth, "to a virgin espoused to a man whose name was Joseph, of the House of David; and the virgin's name was Mary" (Luke 1:27). The angel told her, "Fear not, Mary: for thou hast found favour with God. And, behold, thou shalt conceive in thy womb, and bring forth a son, and shalt call his name JESUS. He shall be great . . . and of his kingdom there shall be no end" (Luke 1:30–33).

The angel of the Lord appears to the shepherds abiding in the field, keeping watch over their flock (see Luke 2:8–9). With the angel's presence, "the glory of the Lord shone round about them: and they were sore afraid" (Luke 2:9). Once again, the angel exclaimed: "Fear not: for, behold, I bring you good tidings of great joy, which shall be to all people. For unto you is born this day in the city of David a Saviour, which is Christ the Lord" (Luke 2:10–11). "And suddenly there was with the angel a multitude of the heavenly host praising God, and saying, Glory to God in the highest, and on earth peace, good will toward men" (Luke 2:13–14).

As we ponder the angels that help us celebrate Christmas, we remember that the birth, life, and infinite sacrifice of Jesus Christ all vanquish fear forever. We too can joyfully echo the heavenly host's praise: "Glory to God in the highest, and on earth peace, good will toward men" (Luke 2:14). Through Jesus Christ, our fear of spiritual and physical death transforms into the hope of forgiveness and a glorious life yet to come.

WHAT IS THE HISTORY OF CHRISTMAS ANGELS?

The exact origin of Christmas angels as ornaments is not known; however, it is believed that Scandinavians were some of the first to fashion such ornaments from materials like straw. Glass blowers in Germany later invented glass angel ornaments to adorn their Christmas trees. Society's ongoing fascination with angels is evident in popular culture as shown by the staying power of the angel, Clarence, in the movie *It's A Wonderful Life,* or by the ghosts of Christmas past, present, and future in *A Christmas Carol.*

"And the angel said unto her, Fear not, Mary: for thou hast found favour with God. And, behold, thou shalt conceive in thy womb, and bring forth a son, and shalt call his name Jesus. He shall be great, and shall be called the Son of the Highest: and the Lord God shall give unto him the throne of his father David: And he shall reign over the house of Jacob for ever; and of his kingdom there shall be no end."

—Luke 1:30–33

Angels testified of Jesus Christ in times of old, and they continue to bear witness of His role as Savior and Redeemer in our modern-day Christmas celebration. A verse from Henry Frances Lyte's poem: "Praise The Lord, O My Soul" reminds us of the crucial role angels played at Christ's birth:

> *Angels, help us to adore him,*
> *Ye behold him face to face;*
> *Sun and moon, bow down before him;*
> *Dwellers all in time and space,*
> *Praise him, praise him.*
> *Praise with us the God of grace.*

WHAT WE HAVE DONE TO FIND TESTIMONIES OF CHRIST IN CHRISTMAS ANGELS

We have carefully collected one angel per year for the thirty-five years of our marriage. As we decorate our home each year for the holiday season, we lovingly place the angels on the mantle above our living room fireplace. We reminisce about each angel and where and how we got it and how that particular angel or the experience finding it causes us to remember Christ. We have one angel carved from olive wood that we brought home from Jerusalem. We have a Lladro angel that we found in a little shop in Seville, Spain. And we treasure an angel that our daughter made for us in her first-grade class at school. Regardless of the materials used to fashion the ornament, we remember special family togetherness that took place in

our search for the "perfect" Christmas angel of each year. Our collection reminds us that Heavenly Father sends real angels to testify of our Savior and to warn, guide, teach, and serve us. Angels are messengers of Jesus Christ. As our family treasures our Christmas angels, we ponder the sacred role of real angels in all shapes, sizes, and varieties.

WHAT YOU CAN DO TO FIND TESTIMONIES OF CHRIST IN CHRISTMAS ANGELS

- Gather and watch a Christmas angel movie such as *It's a Wonderful Life* or *A Christmas Carol*. Talk about angels, who they are, and what their mission is.

- Begin a Christmas angel collection for your family. Add at least one special angel each year that you will display in your home. Discuss the angels of the first Christmas season and how they warn, protect, inform, and guide God's children to Christ, who vanquishes all fear. Invite your family members to help you find one special angel each year.

- Make snow angels together as a family. Then warm up as you discuss angels and the role they play in confirming our testimony of Christ.

- Bake an angel food cake with real whipped cream and fresh strawberries. Discuss how the red and white colors are a beautiful symbol of Christmas and the angel food cake is perfect for the occasion. Enjoy the cake as you sit around your Christmas tree in the warm glow of the lights and talk about angels.

Fluffy Red and White Angel Cake

INGREDIENTS

1¾ cup sugar

¼ teaspoon salt

12 egg whites (room temperature)

1 cup cake flour (sifted)

⅓ cup warm water

1 teaspoon almond or vanilla extract

1½ teaspoons cream of tartar

DIRECTIONS

Preheat oven to 350 degrees. Mix sugar in a blender or food processor until ground very finely. Remove almost one cup of sugar and set aside. Combine salt, cake flour, and remaining sugar, and sift in large bowl.

In a separate bowl, whisk egg whites, water, extract, and cream of tartar until well combined. After a couple of minutes, use a hand mixer to mix in the reserved sugar. Beat at medium speed until you have medium-sized peaks. Sift enough flour onto the top of the mixture to dust the top of the peaks. Fold gently. Continue this process until all flour is incorporated. Be careful not to overwork the mixture.

Spoon mixture into an ungreased Bundt pan. Bake for 35 minutes. Cool upside down for an hour before removing from pan.

Top with strawberries and real whipped cream.

Angel Hair Whipped Cream Topping

INGREDIENTS

1 cup heavy whipping cream

2 Tablespoons powdered sugar

DIRECTIONS

Whisk cream and sugar with a hand mixer until the cream shows stiff peaks. Place on top of cooled angel food cake, top with sliced strawberries, and serve. Refrigerate any remaining whipped cream in an airtight container.

CHAPTER 7

LIGHTS AND CANDLES

HOW DO CHRISTMAS LIGHTS AND CANDLES CONFIRM OUR TESTIMONY OF CHRIST?

Christmas lights and candles bear record of Jesus Christ by reminding us that He is the light of all the world and that it is by His light that we are able to find our way back to our Heavenly home. John declares that Christ is the "true Light, which lighteth every man that cometh into the world" (John 1:9). Jesus taught, "I am come a light into the world, that whosoever believeth on me should not abide in darkness" (John 12:46). It is the light of Christ's example that provides the bright hope for better things to come, the perfect example of righteousness, and the radiant clarity necessary to come to know God the Father and His plan of happiness.

At Christmastime, candles shimmer from windows and snow-covered homes. Colored lights reflect on windowpanes and glow from rooftops and gables with the brilliance of the season. At Christmas, the whole world seems to sparkle its way through icy winter nights. A significant part of the magic of the Christmas experience is to "see the lights." In these lights, we are able to remember that it is Christ that ignites the burning flame of truth and drives away darkness, sin, and confusion. Each flame beckons us to remember the birth of Jesus Christ, the light of the world.

In the words of Washington Irving, "Christmas is a season for kindling the fire for hospitality in the hall, the genial flame of charity in the heart."[9] Whenever we see a Christmas light or flame, we can choose to rekindle our own heartfelt flame of charity.

WHAT IS THE HISTORY OF CHRISTMAS LIGHTS AND CANDLES?

The first Christmas lights were likely small oil lamps used to illuminate the stable where Mary and Joseph welcomed the Son of God into the world. It is possible that the shepherds who came in haste on the night of Christ's birth followed the path to Bethlehem by torch or lantern light. Others, like the Wise Men, were inspired to go in search of Jesus

---

9 Washington Irving, *The Sketch Book*, Geoffrey Crayon, Gent. (New York: G. Putnam, 1857), 237–39.

by the brightness of light, and by the light of a special star they found the Christ child. In honor of those who go in search of the Savior, Christmas has become a celebration of light.

"A Christmas candle is a lovely thing; It makes no noise at all, But softly gives itself away; While quite unselfish, it grows small."

—Eva K. Logue

In medieval times, people sought to transform the long, dark nights of winter into the bright light of day. The symbolic act of burning the Yule log was easily converted into a Christian custom, bringing Christ into one's home to illuminate all who entered (see Matthew 5:14–16). Christians in medieval times chopped down a tree, cut it up, and carried it into their home to burn as a Yule log. The Yule log is a large segment of a tree burned in the fireplace as a part of a traditional Christmas celebration. The log was brought into the home on Christmas Eve, ignited, and allowed to burn throughout the entire holiday celebration.

By the light of the fire, people would tell stories, eat their feast, and watch the glow that emanated from the fireplace.

Other Christmas light traditions developed later, including candles set in windows to signal that those in need could find welcome in that home. The practice of placing candles in the window at Christmas became a symbol of hope for a weary traveler, who like Joseph and Mary, might be in need of shelter. It signaled a willingness to open one's home to others, following the example of Christ and giving freely of one's abundance to those in need.

Much later, in the late 1800s, an employee of Thomas Edison, the inventor of the electric light, brought a strand of lights home with the idea of placing this safer and more practical form of light on his family Christmas tree. The idea was an immediate sensation, and Edward Johnson's family tree became the object of attention from the press and every passerby. Later, another man found substitute lighting in the form of a string of lights taken from a telephone switchboard. Electric Christmas lights emerged as an invention that remains a significant part of our modern-day Christmas celebration.

Thanks to this custom, the practice of decorating with lights during the holiday season brings the glow of the Christmas spirit into our homes. The lights clearly reflect the guiding light of the Savior's example. As Martin Luther observed of Christ, "When He came, there was no light. When He left, there was no darkness."

"Ye are the light of the world. A city that is set on an hill cannot be hid. Neither do men light a candle, and put it under a bushel, but on a candlestick; and it giveth light unto all that are in the house. Let your light so shine before men, that they may see your good works, and glorify your Father which is in heaven."

—Matthew 5:14–16

WHAT WE HAVE DONE TO FIND TESTIMONIES OF CHRIST IN CHRISTMAS LIGHTS AND CANDLES

One Christmas season during a power outage, we drove to the top of a big hill overlooking the community where we live. Suddenly, as we drove along the dark road, a remarkable explosion of light pierced the darkness in a glorious burst of color. The power had returned. Light overcame dark. As we watched the breathtaking light swallow up the darkness, we suddenly knew how the light of our Savior brilliantly overcomes the wickedness of the world. We saw how, on the night of Christ's birth, the light of everlasting truth illuminated an obscure universe. Although there will be times of darkness in this life, the light of Christ will always shine brightly before us.

WHAT YOU CAN DO TO FIND TESTIMONIES OF CHRIST IN CHRISTMAS LIGHTS AND CANDLES

- Identify nearby areas in your community where Christmas lights are abundant, and embark on a Christmas light tour with family and friends. As you drive, discuss how Jesus is the light of the world and the fact that He has asked us to let our light shine (see Matthew 5:16).

- Spend an evening sitting in the light of your own Christmas tree. Sing "O Little Town of Bethlehem," and discuss the how Christ is the "everlasting light."

- Conduct a family candle lighting event in which all members of your family simultaneously light a Christmas candle wherever they may be in the world. Have each person identify at least one way he or she can follow the light of Christ as it leads him or her to help someone in need.

- You might also enjoy lighting a Christmas candle each evening in December on the nights leading up to Christmas. While the candle burns, read Christmas stories, poems, or sing Christmas carols. Extinguish the Christmas candle with the promise to light it again each successive night until Christmas day arrives.

- Prepare some cupcakes and invite your family to help you decorate them with pretty birthday candles. As you talk about how candles and lights remind us of Christ and His birthday, remember to mention that the purpose of the season is to celebrate how His birth brought light to a dark world.

Jesus's Birthday Cupcakes

INGREDIENTS

1 box of your favorite cake mix (our favorite is spice cake)

2 eggs

½ cup vegetable or canola oil

½ cup chocolate chips

DIRECTIONS

Combine cake mix, eggs, and oil in large mixing bowl. Beat. Stir in chocolate chips, and chill for 1 hour. Preheat oven to 350 degrees. Drop batter into prepared muffin tin with paper liners and bake for 7–9 minutes. Frost with cream cheese frosting.

Cream Cheese Frosting

INGREDIENTS

½ cup butter (room temperature)

8 ounces cream cheese

2 teaspoons vanilla extract

4 cups powdered sugar

DIRECTIONS

Cream butter, cream cheese, and vanilla. Add powdered sugar slowly until desired consistency is reached. Spread on top of each cupcake. Enjoy!

CHAPTER 8

STAR

HOW DOES THE CHRISTMAS STAR CONFIRM OUR TESTIMONY OF CHRIST?

The star figures prominently in the account of the Wise Men, who report to Herod that they have seen a star in the east that heralds the birth of the newborn King of the Jews (see Matthew 2:1–2), and the same star leads the Wise Men to Christ (see Matthew 2:9–11).

At Christmastime, our family loves to look for stars of every shape and color. The star bears record of Christ in many ways. The Star of Bethlehem that figures prominently in our Nativity scenes reminds us of our need to search for Jesus and follow His perfect example. Just as the Wise Men of old followed the star's guiding light and were richly rewarded by finding the Christ child, so we will be equally blessed as we recognize the spiritual light that illuminates the covenant path of discipleship, guiding us to our Savior and eternal life.

Our children love to hear a beautiful legend recounted by author C. S. Bailey. It tells of an old grandmother, Babushka, who sits comfortably in her little house on the night the Christ child is born. While she rests calmly by the warm fire, a terrible storm rages outside. Suddenly, she hears a loud rapping at her door. Outside, she sees three white-bearded Wise Men who invite her to join them in their quest to follow the light of the Christmas star to find Christ and bestow gifts upon him. To do so, she must leave the comfort of her cottage and the warm fire by which she rests; she must enter the cold wintry night that leads to an unknown land.

After some thought, she responds: "It is too late to go with you. The weather is too cold. Perhaps later I will go in search of the Christ child when it is light and warm." The next morning after the storm has passed and the journey seems less formidable, she sets out with her own gifts for the baby Jesus. But it is too late. Without the star, she cannot discern which way to go. She mourns her lost opportunity and goes forevermore in search of Christ, unable to find Him. Each year at the time of His birth, she enters softly into all homes where children live, hoping to find Him. "Is He here?" she utters. "Is the little Christ child here?" And then she turns sorrowfully away again, crying: "Further on, further on." Before she leaves each home, she removes a toy from her basket and lays it beside each child's pillow as a Christmas gift. "For His sake," she whispers softly. And then she hurries on, forever in search of the light that leads to the Christ child.

"When they saw the star, they rejoiced with exceeding great joy."

—Matthew 2:10

Fortunately, we need not experience the same sorrow that poor Babushka feels. We can find Christ, but to do so we must, on occasion, abandon the warmth and comforts we enjoy. We must not delay, merely waiting until it is more convenient. Instead, we must immediately and constantly follow the light and signs that lead us safely to Christ.

The faithful who follow the Christmas star in search of Christ will always find Him. These wise men and women accept truth as they encounter it, and they act as the Savior Himself acts: they go about doing good. When we place the star on our Christmas tree or observe other representations of the Star of Bethlehem during the holiday season, we can remember that we too can seek light and truth and immediately do all we can to carry our own precious gifts of personal righteousness and service to lay at the feet of our Redeemer.

WHAT IS THE HISTORY OF THE CHRISTMAS STAR?

We first learn of the Star of Bethlehem in Matthew's account of Jesus's birth. The scriptures explain: "Now when Jesus was born in Bethlehem of Judaea in the days of Herod the king, behold, there came wise men from the east to Jerusalem" (Matthew 2:1). The Star of Bethlehem is of sufficient importance that the Wise Men bring it to the attention of King Herod. The scriptures tell us that "Herod, when he had privily called the wise men, inquired of them diligently what time the star appeared" (Matthew 2:7). It is important to note that apparently, the star is not obvious to all; otherwise, Herod would not have to inquire as to the time of its appearance. The scriptural account never says that Herod saw the star. The star appeared, provided guidance, and then reappeared later, giving additional guidance as needed in order to enable the wise men to find Jesus. Herod's inability to see the guiding light of the star for himself might symbolize that he was not spiritually capable of "seeing the light" and was therefore unable to find the bright guide that leads others to Jesus. In fact, Herod's wickedness may be what prevented him from giving the necessary attention to the sign of Christ's coming; ultimately, his own state of unworthiness may have been what kept him from the blessings that spiritual light offers to true worshipers and followers of Christ. Indeed, Herod tried to use the star to advance his own evil plot to kill the Child King and His family.

In contrast, the Wise Men chose to follow the star in order to worship, to adore, and to bestow gifts upon Jesus Christ. "When they had heard the king, they departed; and, lo, the star, which they saw in the east, went before them, till it came and stood over where the young child was" (Matthew 2:9). Evidently, the sensitivity of the Wise Men to spiritual guidance is the gift that enabled them to be guided by the light of the star when others, such as the corrupt Herod and his scribes and priests, could not. To witness the light of the Star of Bethlehem is to experience joy. The Wise Men followed the star and found joy. "When they saw the star, they rejoiced with exceeding great joy. And when they were come into the house, they saw the young child with Mary his mother, and fell down, and worshipped him" (Matthew 2:10–11).

As we ponder the beautiful, decorative stars that we find everywhere at Christmastime, we may likewise rejoice with exceeding great joy and fall before our Redeemer and worship Him, presenting to Him our precious gifts of repentance, commitment to the principles of the gospel, covenant making and keeping, and daily personal righteousness. May we avoid the Herod-like evil elements so prevalent in our world today, which work to destroy the family. From such, we must turn away. Only then will we be able to focus on the guiding lights of truth that silently guide us to our Savior.

WHAT WE HAVE DONE TO FIND TESTIMONIES OF CHRIST IN THE CHRISTMAS STAR

Each Christmas season, we choose a special evening to gather our family on the back deck of our home to stargaze. On a crisp, clear winter night, we make hot chocolate, bundle in blankets, and try to identify the constellations we can see from our backyard. Sometimes we are fortunate enough to see a falling star or catch a glimpse of a fast-moving satellite, but central to every stargazing experience is a discussion of the Star of Bethlehem and how God sent light from heaven to guide the faithful Wise Men to the Christ child. Over the years, we have discussed the heavenly signs and wonders that were present at the time of our Savior's birth. We have also discussed how miraculous it is that our loving Heavenly

Father knew to place the Star of Bethlehem in its very particular orbit eons before its starlight would need to shine so brightly as to guide Wise Men to Christ. Starlight travels at 186,000 miles per second, taking years to reach us. Yet our loving Heavenly Father perfectly planned the arrival of light to guide Wise Men to Jesus. Likewise He delivers light to guide each of us throughout our mortal sojourn. We testify that God knows the beginning and the end and that He loves us eternally.

WHAT YOU CAN DO TO FIND TESTIMONIES OF CHRIST IN THE CHRISTMAS STAR

- Conduct a family Star of Bethlehem activity in which you select a clear night in December to gather your family outside to stargaze. You may want to prepare hot cocoa and have plenty of blankets for snuggling. Discuss the star and how its light is a loving beacon that leads those who are searching for Christ.

- Lead a family discussion about what each member of your family might do in order to follow the Star of Bethlehem and go in search of Christ. Be sure to explain that as wise men and women, we must not object to giving up the comforts of complacency.

- Make homemade, star-shaped marshmallows. Different sizes and colors make it especially fun. Have a family member prepare a lesson about the Star of Bethlehem. Discuss how the star carries our thoughts to Christ as you make and eat your marshmallows. Prepare some creamy cocoa with which to enjoy the chewy treats.

Magi Marshmallows

INGREDIENTS

    3 packages of unflavored gelatin

    ½ cup cold water

    1½ cups sugar

    1 cup light corn syrup

    ¼ teaspoon salt

    ½ cup water

    1 Tablespoon vanilla extract

    2–3 drops of red or green food coloring (optional)

DIRECTIONS

Combine gelatin and cold water using a hand mixer while you make the syrup: Combine the sugar, corn syrup, salt, and ½ cup water in a small saucepan and cook over medium heat. Once sugar dissolves, raise heat to high and cook to 240 degrees F on a candy thermometer. Remove from heat. Leave whisk mixer on low speed and slowly add syrup to gelatin mixture. Move mixer to high speed and whip until very thick (10–15 minutes). Add vanilla and mix well.

Dust a non-metal baking dish with powdered sugar. Pour marshmallow mixture over pan and smooth out the top. Finish by dusting powdered sugar over the top of the marshmallow mixture. Let stand overnight uncovered until dried out. Flip marshmallow out on cutting board and use a star shaped cookie-cutter to cut it into star shapes. Float these dreamy marshmallows in your own favorite hot chocolate recipe, and drink in the goodness.

CHAPTER 9

WREATH

HOW DOES THE CHRISTMAS WREATH CONFIRM OUR TESTIMONY OF CHRIST?

Each Christmas, we decorate our doors, windows, and even our tables with brightly colored wreaths. The Christmas wreath represents the eternal round that the scriptures reference when defining eternity, the path that has no beginning or end. Because the Christmas wreath's greenery survives the cold of winter, it also helps us to think about the amazing promise of everlasting life that the Atonement provides.

The wreath also reminds us of the crown of thorns placed on Jesus's head at the time of His Crucifixion. It symbolizes His willingness to suffer all manner of pain and mockery to complete His mission of mercy (see Matthew 27:29). The crown-shaped wreath symbolizes Christ's elevated status as the Lord of lords and King of kings, who was victorious over death and sin and who shall reign triumphantly throughout all eternity (see Revelation 17:14). The Christmas wreath signifies Christ's spiritual victory over sin and His physical victory over death.

Finally, the wreath helps us to remember that Jesus will return and wear another crown—not of thorns, but a halo of glory as the King of heaven and earth. For those who fight the good fight and keep the faith in Him, there awaits a crown of righteousness, which can be represented by the Christmas wreath (see 2 Timothy 4:7–8). This crown awaits all those who love Him. Whenever you see a Christmas wreath, remember to see the crown of Christ the King.

WHAT IS THE HISTORY OF THE CHRISTMAS WREATH?

The word *wreath* comes from an English term meaning "to writhe or twist." Wreaths are formed by twisting boughs into fragrant rings of evergreen, holly, pine, spruce, or fir. In ancient times, Greeks and Romans formed crown-like wreaths as awards to athletes and military heroes. Because of this practice, the wreath became a symbol of victory, worn as a crown. Later, royalty began to fashion now-familiar jewel-covered crowns in the shape of the ancient victory wreath.

The modern-day Christmas wreath may also trace some of its origins to the Swedish crown of lights worn by young girls on Saint Lucia's Day. According to legend, Lucia was a beautiful young Christian girl who gave her dowry to the poor. She delivered bread and other food to impoverished Swedes when they needed it most. Now, each December, the Swedes—and many others around the world—honor her memory. The annual tradition is for young girls to dress in white dresses with red sashes. Usually, the oldest daughter in the family places on her head a crown made of a leafy wreath topped by lighted candles. Dressed as Lucia, she serves special bread to her family.

This Swedish tradition may also give rise to an additional tradition known as the Advent wreath. Families prepare the Advent wreath with evergreen boughs, sometimes trimmed with pinecones, ribbons, and candles. The term *advent* derives from the Latin *adventus*, which means "a coming." The Advent season reminds all Christians of the birth of the Savior, which was the first advent or coming. Advent begins on the Sunday nearest November 30. According to tradition, the Advent wreath consists of four to five candles—one rose-colored, one white, and three purple. Each of the purple and rose candles are fastened at spaced intervals around the wreath with the white candle placed in the middle. The royal-colored purple candles symbolize hope, peace, and love. The family lights the purple candles on the first, second, and fourth Sundays of December. The family lights the rose-colored candle, which represents joy, on the third Sunday. On Christmas Eve and Christmas Day, the family replaces the colored candles with white candles to represent the purity of Christ. The candles burn while the family reads scriptures or sings hymns to invite a solemn spirit of worship to the home. It offers a reminder to focus on the hope, peace, love, joy, and purity that Christ brought to the world.

WHAT WE HAVE DONE TO FIND TESTIMONIES OF CHRIST IN THE CHRISTMAS WREATH

One Christmas our youngest son, with help from his first-grade schoolteacher, made a ceramic Christmas wreath as his special Christmas gift for us. He formed it carefully and then baked it to seal its shape. He painted it with bright green paint, and then he created small berries that he colored red and glued to the rest of the piece to create the perfect holly berry wreath. That little ornament is a family treasure. Each year when we hang it on our Christmas tree, we smile and remember how excited our son was to present it to us and to explain the symbolism associated with the Christmas wreath and the Christmas colors of red and green. That little Christmas memory continues to live in our hearts and minds every time we see the sweet, wreath-shaped ornament.

"Perhaps the best Yuletide decoration is being wreathed in smiles."

– Unknown

WHAT YOU CAN DO TO FIND TESTIMONIES OF CHRIST IN THE CHRISTMAS WREATH

• Invite your family to help as you hang your wreath(s). Discuss the ways the wreath reminds you of Christ as you decide where to hang it. Choose a special place where all who enter your home will see it and enjoy its beauty and symbolism. Don't hesitate to explain its significance to all who visit your home.

• Plan a wreath activity similar to the Advent wreath activity we shared earlier. Prepare a tabletop wreath and place four candles (one pink and three purple) in the wreath. Plan to take a few minutes as a family each Sunday in December to light one of the candles and discuss the significance of the candle, using scriptures as a resource:

◦ As you light the "Hope" candle on the first Sunday, discuss your family's expectations and wishes for the Christmas season. Remind your family that we find true hope for salvation and lasting happiness only in the gospel.

◦ On the second Sunday, light the "Peace" candle and talk about the peace we can feel at Christmas as we consider the life of our Savior. Invite each family member to promise to go about doing good as Jesus did.

◦ On the third Sunday, light the "Joy" candle and celebrate the joy we can all experience knowing that Christ was born, lived a perfect life, atoned for our sins, and made the universal resurrection possible. It was Jesus who admonished all of us to "be of good cheer" and to "be not afraid" even in the most difficult of times (Mark 6:50).

◦ On Christmas Eve and Christmas Day, light the white candle and discuss the need to keep the commandments and remain pure and virtuous.

◦ On the final Sunday of the month, light the "Love" candle, and remind your family that God so loved the world that He gave us His only begotten Son (see John 3:16). Invite each family member to make the solemn promise to show love for Jesus Christ by keeping His commandments, sharing His gospel, and being kind and loving toward all mankind.

- Make some wreath treats and share them with anyone who comes to visit. Always take the opportunity to explain how the wreath bears record of the Savior.
- A Christmas wreath Bundt cake is also a festive and fun treat to help teach how the wreath testifies of Christ.

Puffed Rice Christmas Wreath Yummies

Ingredients

½ cup (1 stick) butter

1 cup corn syrup

1 pound brown sugar

1 can sweetened condensed milk

1 teaspoon vanilla

Green food coloring

6 cups puffed rice cereal

1 bag Red Hots candies

Directions

Combine butter, corn syrup, and brown sugar in a saucepan, and bring to a boil. Add condensed milk. Cook to soft-ball stage; add vanilla. Add green food coloring. Pour over puffed rice; mix well, and shape into wreaths. Put on wax paper to set. Add three Red Hots candies to each wreath to look like berries.

Christmas Wreath Bundt Cake

Ingredients

1 box of your favorite cake mix

Red and green frosting

Directions

Bake cake in Bundt pan as directed on box. Let cool; remove from pan onto a cake plate or prepared serving tray.

Decorate the cake using red and green frosting. Use Ziploc bags and a star piping tip to create a wreath look. Use a flat tip to create a beautiful red bow.

CHAPTER 10

GINGERBREAD AND OTHER BAKED GOODS

HOW DO GINGERBREAD AND OTHER BAKED GOODS CONFIRM OUR TESTIMONY OF CHRIST?

Gingerbread is a treat that people all around the world enjoy. We have come to associate the delicious aroma and sweet spice of ginger with Christmas. Making gingerbread houses and cookies is one of our family's favorite Christmas traditions. For us, preparing, sharing, and partaking of these special Christmas gingerbreads and other baked goods bear record of Jesus, who describes Himself as the "bread of life" (John 6:35). Whenever we give or receive Christmas baked goods, we can remember the promises we make each week as we partake of the sacramental bread and renew our baptismal covenants with our Heavenly Father. It is remarkable that these simple gifts can remind us to come unto Christ and be partakers of Him, the Bread of Life.

Bethlehem, interpreted, means "house of bread," and its modern name, *Beit-Lahm*, means "house of flesh." The town of Christ's birthplace no doubt takes its name from its rich fields, where Ruth gathered grains and other sustenance and where Naomi discovered the path to return to her home. It was in Bethlehem that King David was born and anointed King. Most importantly, prophets testified long before Christ's birth that He "whose goings forth have been from of old" would be born in Bethlehem (Micah 5:2).

With His humble beginnings in the "house of bread," it is fitting then that Jesus declared, "I am the living bread which came down from heaven: if any man eat of this bread, he shall live forever: and the bread that I will give is my flesh, which I will give for the life of the world" (John 6:51). In this clear reference to Christ's willingness to sacrifice His body, Jesus explains that those who partake of His Atonement through repentance and covenant keeping shall enjoy eternal life.

WHAT IS THE HISTORY OF CHRISTMAS GINGERBREAD?

During the Middle Ages in England, gingerbread simply meant any bread, cake, or pastry that was preserved with the ginger spice. During the time of King Richard, soldiers returned to England from the crusades with sugars and spices that they discovered in the Middle East.

Gingerbread's a lovely treat.
It always smells so sweet.
It takes my thoughts to Christ the Lord.
It gives me food to eat.
This festive bread's a symbol true that
God commenced as man.
In Bethlehem, the house of bread, His
humble life began.

Gingerbread's a custom sure
that started long ago
To be a Christmas gift of love
and teaches me to know
That Christ the Lord has now become
my only bread of life
From Him I gain the strength to fight
through mortal pain and strife.

Gingerbread is so much more
than sustenance for me.
It helps me think of Calvry's cross and of
Gethsemane.
It guides my thoughts unto His tomb
wherein His body lay,
Until He triumphed over death
to pave for me the way.

— Larry and Lisa Laycock

The people used these sugars and spices to bake sweet gingerbreads. In one interesting legend, young girls in England made it a tradition to eat gingerbread men, or "husbands," to ensure that they would be able to fulfill their hope and dream to be married during the coming year.

Gingerbread became a traditional sweet to be shared during the Christmas holiday when bakers began to form Christmas shapes from the brown dough, including houses, stars, angels, and Christmas trees. Legend also tells that Queen Victoria and her husband, Albert, included gingerbread cookies and other pastries of German origin in their celebration of Christmas. Soon gingerbread became popular in England and America as treats and decorations. For this reason, it is not unusual to use gingerbread cookies as decorations on Christmas trees.

WHAT WE HAVE DONE TO FIND TESTIMONIES OF CHRIST IN CHRISTMAS GINGERBREAD

One year, we had to leave town in early December, so we invited Larry's mom to come and stay with our kids while we were away. When she arrived, she was like Mary Poppins, magically pulling all sorts of fun Christmas activities out of her carpetbag. Our kids were delighted when they saw the gingerbread house kit she had carefully concealed in her satchel. She retrieved baggies full of colorful Christmas candies that they would use to decorate their gingerbread house. Our kids couldn't wait for us to leave so that they could get busy having fun with Grandma. We received pictures of all the kids covered from head to foot in icing and sweets after they had decorated the gingerbread house. The kitchen looked

like the North Pole, completely covered in white icing snow. But through the colored chaos, our children's faces radiated wonder and joy. Their eyes danced, and they will never forget that family gingerbread activity with Grandma.

WHAT YOU CAN DO TO FIND TESTIMONIES OF CHRIST IN GINGERBREAD AND OTHER BAKED GOODS

- Devote time to conduct a family baking activity. Prepare gingerbread men, a gingerbread house, or other Christmas baked goods as a gift for neighbors or friends. While rolling out the dough and baking the gingerbread, explain that *Bethlehem* means "house of bread." Then explain that this is a fitting name for the birthplace of Christ, who is the Bread of Life (see John 6).

- Make and decorate a gingerbread house together. Remind everyone that Christmas baked goods truly bear record of our Savior, who laid down His body to make it possible for us to be cleansed of our sins. Ponder together how partaking of the sacrament bread reminds us that Christ is the Bread of Life. One year, we prepared a gingerbread house for each child. Then we spent an evening decorating them. We laughed and talked about how Jesus is the Bread of Life. Then we awarded prizes for different gingerbread achievements: the most creative, the best use of color, the ugliest, and on and on.

- Bake gingerbread cookies, and retell the story of Jesus's birth in the city known as the house of bread as you roll and cut them.

Gingerbread Cookies

INGREDIENTS

6 cups all-purpose flour

1 Tablespoon baking powder

1 teaspoon salt

½ teaspoon allspice

½ teaspoon ground cloves

1 teaspoon ground ginger

¼ teaspoon ground nutmeg

1 teaspoon ground cinnamon

1 cup butter (melted) and cooled

1 cup firmly packed brown sugar

1 cup molasses

2 whole eggs

½ cup water

Powdered sugar (for topping)

½ cup large-grain sugar (for topping)

DIRECTIONS

In a large bowl, combine flour, baking powder, salt, allspice, cloves, ginger, nutmeg, and cinnamon. Set aside.

In a large mixer, combine butter and brown sugar. Add molasses slowly and then add eggs and water until mixed well. Add flour mixture to butter mixture, until all absorbed.

Refrigerate dough in plastic wrap for 3 hours or more. When it is time to bake the cookies, preheat oven to 350 degrees, remove dough from fridge, and roll out on floured surface to ¼ inch. Use cookie cutters to make desired shapes, and place on baking sheet. Bake for 10–12 minutes. Cookies should still be soft and appear dry. Top with powdered sugar or large-grain sugar. You can also ice with your favorite icing and decorate with candies.

CHAPTER 11

MUSIC

HOW DOES CHRISTMAS MUSIC CONFIRM OUR TESTIMONY OF CHRIST?

Music is an essential element of the Christmas celebration. Old familiar hymns playing softly around us at Christmastime carry our thoughts far away to angels we have heard on high, to silent holy nights where mangers are filled with hay, and even to joyous bells of Christmas Day. More modern Christmas music helps us treasure silver bells, being home for Christmas, and the breath of heaven. Popular Christmas hymns and songs bear record of Christ through inspired lyrics and instrumental accompaniments that lead our thoughts and hearts to heaven.

At the time of Christ's birth, there were shepherds "abiding in the field, keeping watch over their flock by night" in a powerful, symbolic representation of our Good Shepherd's careful watch over us during this mortal probation (Luke 2:8). The angel of the Lord appeared to the shepherds and "the glory of the Lord shone round about them" (Luke 2:9). The angel brought tidings of great joy to all people and then "suddenly there was with the angel a multitude of the heavenly host praising God, and saying, Glory to God in the highest, and on earth peace, good will toward men" (Luke 2:13–14). When the shepherds heard that first Christmas carol, it changed them forever.

Music, in the form of the angels' song of praise, announced the long-awaited arrival of the Savior of all the world, bringing peace and goodwill, reconciliation between God and man. Music is the universal language that bears record of Christ to a searching world.

WHAT IS THE HISTORY OF CHRISTMAS MUSIC?

The legends behind some of the popular music we hear at Christmas most certainly bear record of the living Christ. For example, in a miraculous turn of events, a broken church organ gave Joseph Mohr the incentive he needed to combine his lyrics with guitar music that his friend Franz Gruber composed. On the night of the broken organ performance, Mohr collaborated with Gruber, and backed by a small church choir, the two performed one of the most loved Christmas hymns of all time, "Silent Night," for the first time. The gentle hymn is now sung in more than 140 languages throughout the world. Whenever we sing or hear it, our thoughts turn to Christ and His humble birth.

*"Then let your hearts
be filled with joy,
While Christmas bells
are ringing,
And keep the birthday
of the Lord
With Merriment and
singing."*

—Mary Jane Carr

We find another example of the divine origin of a beloved Christmas hymn in the recounting of the experience of preacher Phillip Brooks. Brooks made a pilgrimage from Jerusalem to Bethlehem in 1856 in order to attend the Church of the Nativity celebration. On that starry night, beautiful Bethlehem inspired the young preacher to write a tribute to the holy birthplace of our Lord: "O Little Town of Bethlehem." As we sing or listen to this familiar hymn, we remember that in Bethlehem's dark streets "shineth the everlasting Light" and that "the hopes and fears of all the years are met in [Bethlehem] tonight." The hymn transports our thoughts and hearts to Christ.

Even seemingly secular music testifies of Christ if we pay close attention. One of our family's favorite legends is the explanation of how "The Twelve Days of Christmas" may have been composed. The legend says that in sixteenth-century England, wicked leaders prevented many Christians from practicing their religion. During that period, a royal decree forced those who did not embrace a particular religious ideology to take their worship into hiding. Violation of the laws of the time could result in severe punishment, even death. But these persecuted, humble followers of Christ are believed to have found a secret way to express their adoration for our Savior. By carefully hiding doctrinal teaching in cleverly crafted, seemingly harmless lyrics, they could conceal a coded message of their belief and faith. So the "true love" in the song is actually thought to be Christ, who provides all that is essential in this life for His faithful followers. And the twelve days of Christmas are the days between Christmas and Epiphany, the day when the Magi, according to legend, are believed to have found the Christ Child.

For most people, "The Twelve Days of Christmas" is a silly song that simply mentions a series of extravagant gifts that a lovesick man or woman gives to his or her beloved at Christmastime. The song is nonsensical to a modern-day listener who is not hearing with spiritual ears; however, when you seek Christ, even this amusing little Christmas song can transform into a stunning, symbolic message and testimony of the Savior.

Consider the possible hidden testimony that can be found in each gift. Ponder the words, and search for the symbolic meaning that might be hidden. Look for the doctrine of Christ as you consider the unusual gifts.

A Partridge in a Pear Tree

Think of the qualities of a partridge. The mother partridge is known for her selfless sacrifice. When confronted with a mortal enemy, the mother bird will quickly sacrifice herself and protect her chicks by luring the enemy away. Think of Jesus and His selfless sacrifice to save us from sin and death. If the partridge represents Jesus, the pear tree must certainly represent the cross on which he hung. In the song's very first gift, we can discern the voluntary, atoning sacrifice of our Lord.

Two Turtle Doves

Think of the universal symbol of a dove. Doves commonly represent truth and peace. Christians find both truth and peace in the teachings found in the Old and New Testament. The two turtledoves remind us of the love we feel from Jehovah (Christ) of the Old Testament and Jesus (Christ) of the New Testament. We find the doves of truth and peace in our knowledge of God and in His eternal plan of salvation as found in the holy scriptures.

Three French Hens

Ponder the French hen. This once-expensive item represents food fit for a king. The three French hens may remind us of the very expensive gifts that the Magi provided for the Christ Child: gold, frankincense, and myrrh. Just as the Magi offered Christ their best,

most expensive gifts, the song can remind us that we too should give our very best, most valuable gifts to serve and honor Christ.

Four Calling Birds

Think of calling birds. They use their God-given voices to call out warnings that will save the lives of their families and friends. The four calling birds in the song may represent the four Gospel writers that continually call us to the safety and protection we find in being faithful followers of Christ. Matthew, Mark, Luke, and John call out their warning for all to come unto Christ.

Five Gold Rings

Consider five beautiful golden rings. They are of great value. They are desirable. They are in the shape of eternity. The five gold rings might symbolize the law of the Old Testament, or the first five books of the Bible, known as the Torah. The five rings can bind us eternally to Christ if we choose to accept and cherish Him and His commandments found there.

Six Geese a-Laying

Think of six geese laying eggs, or creating new life. Now reflect on the six days used to create the earth. The Lord created the world in six creative periods referred to as days, and He rested on the seventh. Since eggs are a clear symbol of creation and life, the six geese a-laying might be representative of the six creative periods. From the six geese-a-laying, we learn to accept Christ as the Creator of the earth.

Seven Swans a-Swimming

Think of the beauty and grace of a swimming swan. Now compare that to the seven gifts of the Holy Spirit that Paul writes of in Romans 12:6–8. The seven swans in the song may represent the seven gifts of the Holy Spirit that come to us through the Holy Ghost. They include prophesy, ministering or service, teaching, preaching or exhorting, simple giving, presiding or leadership with diligence, and mercy with cheerfulness. The seven gifts of the Spirit can enable us to be like the seven swimming swans—graceful creatures who reflect the Savior's love and goodness.

Eight Maids a-Milking

Consider the job of the milkmaid in ancient times. Hers was one of the most humble of all the tasks performed in the Lord's manor. Now think of the eight beatitudes that the Savior taught in His Sermon on the Mount found in Matthew 5. The milkmaid can be a reminder of the meekness and humility reflected in the eight beatitudes. The eight maids a-milking can remind us to be humble, faithful followers of Christ and His word.

Nine Ladies Dancing

Picture nine graceful ladies dancing in total unison and harmony. Now ponder the fruits of the Spirit as referenced in Galatians 5:22–23. These graceful dancing ladies in the song well represent the fruits of the Spirit that include love, joy, peace, long-suffering or patience, gentleness, goodness, faith, meekness, and temperance or self-restraint. These fruits of the Spirit and Christlike attributes will help us to become like the Savior.

Ten Lords a-Leaping

Think of the term *lord*. The lord of the English manor was a man of honor and the final voice of authority in any decision made there. Hence, the ten lords a-leaping might represent the Ten Commandments of our Lord and the governing influence that these commandments should be in our lives (see Exodus 20). As we obey the Ten Commandments, we can show our love for and devotion to Christ (see John 14:15).

Eleven Pipers Piping

Think of the significance of the number eleven. Of the Twelve Apostles, eleven remained faithful to the end. Each of these spent their lives in service of the Master. The eleven faithful Apostles followed the Lord's charge to proclaim the gospel to all men. They did not become a quorum of twelve again until Mathias was called (see Acts 1). The eleven pipers piping can remind us that we must all be missionaries that spread the gospel throughout the world and invite others to come unto Christ (see Matthew 28:19–20).

Twelve Drummers Drumming

The final gift of twelve drummers drumming may represent the apostolic creed taught to many Christian children. Its twelve points of doctrine span the birth, life, and teachings of Christ, including His Resurrection. As we study the life of Christ, we will become more like Him and will be prepared for eternal life.

WHAT WE HAVE DONE TO FIND TESTIMONIES OF CHRIST IN CHRISTMAS MUSIC

In the recent past, our children and their spouses secretly planned a remarkable Christmas concert for us. They called us together on Christmas Eve in our home and performed their concert wearing their matching Christmas pajamas. We laughed and cried all the way through the program, and we recorded it for future family viewing, entertainment, and worship. It was truly the most magical, inspiring, best Christmas gift they could ever have given us. They each used their talents to share testimony of our Savior and His birth, life, and mission. They recited excerpts from the scriptures. They sang and played instruments in wonderful worship. Our family love grew, and our testimonies increased. This tradition continues each year in our family and is the source of much joy and happiness while family members plan and prepare and present gifts of musical worship.

WHAT YOU CAN DO TO FIND TESTIMONIES OF CHRIST IN CHRISTMAS MUSIC

- We invite you to conduct your own family concert dedicated to worshiping Jesus Christ. Invite each listener to commit to consider the Christmas spirit and the love of God as they listen and participate. Your program can be as simple as one song, sung on someone's front porch, or it can be as grand as arranging a flash mob rendition of Handel's *Messiah* in a local mall.

- Take your family Christmas caroling. Print the lyrics to your favorite Christmas songs. You can go to as many or as few homes as you like to sing and share the Spirit through music.

- Prepare some delicious Christmas wassail and Crock-Pot chili. Sing together as a family "Here We Come A-Caroling (Wassail Song)" and other traditional Christmas songs, and discuss the ways your favorite Christmas music helps you think of Christ.

Wonderful Wassail

INGREDIENTS

    1 cup sugar

    ¼ teaspoon ground ginger

    1½ cinnamon sticks

    ½ teaspoon allspice

    1 cup water

    1 quart orange juice

    2½ quarts apple juice/cider

    ½ large bottle lemon juice

DIRECTIONS

Mix dry ingredients. Simmer in water until the sugar dissolves, stirring constantly. Add remaining liquids to sugar mixture. Heat without boiling. Serve warm. You can keep the wassail in a warm Crock-Pot on low for 4 hours, filling your home with a beautiful Christmas aroma.

Favorite Christmas Chili

INGREDIENTS

    2 cans chicken, drained

    1 16-ounce jar medium salsa

    1 can pinto beans

    1 can red kidney beans (undrained)

    2 cans white northern beans (undrained)

    1 large can corn

    1 large can diced green chilis

    1 package taco seasoning dry mix

    1 package ranch dressing dry mix

    1 pinch garlic salt

DIRECTIONS

Combine ingredients in Crock-Pot, and cook on low 4–6 hours.

Enjoy with cheese, sour cream, and chips or in bread bowls.

CHAPTER 12

MISTLETOE, HOLLY, IVY

HOW DO MISTLETOE, HOLLY, AND IVY CONFIRM OUR TESTIMONY OF CHRIST?

Mistletoe is an evergreen plant that features prominently in many Christmas celebrations. We smile about meeting or kissing under the mistletoe, and we find joy in this fun and festive practice. Mistletoe represents an opportunity for us to express love and affection, and we know our Savior rejoices when we love one another and show our love in word and deed. Think of the Savior's words to His Apostles when he said, "These things I command you, that ye love one another" (John 15:17) and, "By this shall all men know that ye are my disciples, if ye have love one to another" (John 13:35).

As we share our love through an embrace and a kiss under the mistletoe, remember that there is no greater love than the love of our Heavenly Father for us, His children. He gave us His Son to save us from sin and death. Through Christ's willing sacrifice, He demonstrated His ultimate love for us, His friends (see John 15:13). The mistletoe is a beautiful symbol that can help us remember the love of God.

In addition to mistletoe, holly and ivy are also recognized Christmas evergreens that bear testimony of the Lord. The holly and ivy not only have the capacity to retain their vibrant green color during the long days of winter, reminding us of everlasting life, but they also bear fruit throughout the winter while most other plants lie dormant and lifeless. The holly and ivy reflect Christ's teaching that "a good tree cannot bring forth evil fruit, neither can a corrupt tree bring forth good fruit. . . . Wherefore by their fruits ye shall know them" (Matthew 7:18, 20). If we choose to let them, the holly and the ivy can remind all of us that we should bear good fruit—or, in other words, ensure that good works are the essence of our existence and that the fruits of our labors yield a harvest of kindness, service, love, and commitment. The holly bears an additional witness of our Savior: like the wreath, the leaves and berries of the holly are reminiscent of the crown of thorns worn by Christ at His Crucifixion. The red berries represent the drops of precious blood that He freely spilt for our salvation.

WHAT IS THE HISTORY OF THE MISTLETOE, HOLLY, AND IVY TRADITIONS?

Holly and ivy enjoy a long history of symbolism relating to a variety of doctrines, ranging from healing and forgiveness to the eternal family. In addition to representing the

"'Tis merry 'neath the mistletoe,
When holly berries glisten bright;
When Christmas fires gleam and glow,
when wintry winds so wildly blow,
and all the meadows round are white
—'tis merry 'neath the mistletoe!
A privilege 'tis then, you know,
To exercise time honored rite;
When Christmas fires gleam and glow,
When loving lips
may pout although
With other lips they oft unite
—'Tis merry 'neath the mistletoe!"

—J. Ashby Sterry

power to overcome the death of winter, holly and ivy are the subjects of many beautiful legends. According to ancient traditions, families kept both holly and ivy in their homes to receive the complete blessings of prosperity and health during the coming year. The holly was considered to be masculine, while the ivy represented femininity. The combination of the holly and the ivy, as with the union of a man and woman, was considered necessary to complete the cycle of life and happiness in the family.

The legend of the mistletoe dates back to the time of the ancient Celtic druids, who believed the plant to have medicinal power to restore life and cure illness. In another legend, the mistletoe was a statuesque tree that was used as the cross to crucify Christ. Legend explains that after the Crucifixion, God punished the mistletoe tree and reduced it to a lowly shrub and parasitic plant.

In yet another legend, believers hung mistletoe from the lintel posts and doorways of their homes as a sign of their willingness to forgive and make peace with their enemies. To see mistletoe hanging from a neighbor's doorway was an invitation to obtain forgiveness for wrongs and to renew bonds of friendship. This ancient practice, no doubt, gave rise to our current custom, in which mistletoe beckons all to embrace and kiss under its magical boughs.

WHAT WE HAVE DONE TO FIND TESTIMONIES OF CHRIST IN MISTLETOE, HOLLY, AND IVY

Mistletoe has always been a fun part of our family Christmas gatherings. One of our cherished memories is visiting Lisa's Grandmother Gleave's home at Christmas and being welcomed by a giant ball of mistletoe tied with a gorgeous red ribbon with dangling streamers. The festive greenery always waited patiently over the front door for any unsuspecting visitor to pass beneath it. Everyone who entered the home was required to linger under the mistletoe and wait for someone to free him or her with a kiss. It was a small and simple

tradition, but the happy memories of the laughter and fun that came from it will be with us forever. We always remembered Christ and His love as we kissed beneath the mistletoe.

WHAT YOU CAN DO TO FIND TESTIMONIES OF CHRIST IN MISTLETOE, HOLLY, AND IVY

- Hold a small family ceremony when you hang your mistletoe. Call your family together and explain the ancient legend of the mistletoe and that hanging it on your doorway would have been a sign of your willingness to forgive your enemies. Discuss the way in which the holly, ivy, and mistletoe bear record of the Savior's loving forgiveness and Atonement that provide us the opportunity to be redeemed from our sins and enjoy eternal life as families.

- Give each family member or friend a sprig of mistletoe and invite him or her to follow the example of Jesus Christ by expressing willingness to forgive others and love their enemies (see Matthew 5:44–46).

- Bake some peanut butter kiss cookies as a family. Decide on a neighbor that you would like to serve. Wrap the cookies with a sprig of mistletoe and make a card that says: "Merry Kissmas!" Write the legend of the mistletoe and how it testifies of Christ on the card. Deliver the gift as a family and ring the doorbell. Run away before they answer. Your family will enjoy this secret giving experience.

Chocolate Kiss Peanut Butter Cookies

INGREDIENTS

½ cup sugar

½ cup packed brown sugar

½ cup creamy peanut butter

½ cup (1 stick) butter

1 egg

1½ cups flour

¾ teaspoon baking soda

½ teaspoon cinnamon

¼ teaspoon pumpkin pie spice

¼ teaspoon nutmeg

1 bag of chocolate or white chocolate Hershey's Kisses (or Hugs)

DIRECTIONS

Preheat oven to 375 degrees. Beat sugar, brown sugar, peanut butter, butter, and egg with electric mixer at medium speed until blended. Stir in dry ingredients; mix until blended. Shape into walnut-sized balls, roll in sugar, and place on ungreased baking sheet. Bake 8–10 minutes or until edges are lightly brown. Immediately after removing from the oven, press a chocolate into the middle of each cookie and allow to cool on cooling rack.

CHAPTER 13

CANDY CANE

HOW DOES THE CANDY CANE CONFIRM OUR TESTIMONY OF CHRIST?

The candy cane has become a welcome participant in many Christmas celebrations. We almost always receive a candy cane as we visit Santa or empty the contents of overflowing Christmas stockings. When we see the familiar cane-shaped, red-and-white candy, we immediately think of Christmas and all the delicious sweets that accompany the holidays. But the candy cane is much more than just another treat. The candy cane bears record of Jesus Christ through its crook-like shape and red-and-white stripes. It reminds us of Christ's exclamation that He is the Good Shepherd (see John 10:11). Christ reminds us that a good shepherd will give his life for his sheep. As we share candy canes, let us remember to also share our testimony of the Good Shepherd who gave His life for us. As His sheep, or humble followers, let us recognize His voice and give way to His gentle prodding, always allowing Him to gather us in and protect us from danger. The candy cane's shape reminds us that Jesus is the sacrificial "Lamb of God" (John 1:29) and that the lambs offered as a sacrifice at the Feast of the Passover were merely representative of the true Lamb of God, whose holy Atonement fulfilled the law of Moses and provided the promised redemption.

The bold white stripes of the Christmas candy cane bear record of our Savior's purity and His perfect life. The beautiful red stripes speak to us of His precious blood that He sacrificed to pay the price for our sins. The sweetness of the candy cane reminds us to never substitute evil for good—or bitter for sweet, as Isaiah warned would happen in the last days (see Isaiah 5:20).

WHAT IS THE HISTORY OF THE CANDY CANE?

The legend of the origin of the candy cane is found in the oft-told story of a priest who was charged with the responsibility to oversee a children's choir. Tasked with the assignment to assure their good behavior during a Christmas service, he began to ponder how he could accomplish this important task. In a stroke of brilliance, the priest decided to give each child a piece of candy that would not only last a long time but also please the children. In order to give the hard candy a purpose beyond mere pleasure, he petitioned a candy maker to fashion the sweets in the shape of a shepherd's crook so that the children would remember the Good Shepherd. Later, an inspired candy maker added the red and white stripes to remind all who partook of our Savior's purity and atoning blood. So the candy cane became a wise solution to a priest's concern for the behavior of a children's choir and an enduring symbol of Christ and Christmas.

Later, as the candy cane became a popular Christmas gift, it also became a treasured decoration for Christmas trees, wreathes, and homes. Each time we see a candy cane, our thoughts and hearts can turn to our beloved Savior.

WHAT WE HAVE DONE TO FIND TESTIMONIES OF CHRIST IN THE CANDY CANE

O how we love the candy cane
with stripes of white and red!
The crimson bands bring thoughts of
Christ, His blood so freely shed.

The white reminds us of His love
and that He died so pure.
It helps us think of all we know
that makes His love so sure.

The shape is like the shepherd's crook
that gathers in His sheep.
He is our Shepherd night and day,
a careful watch He'll keep.

We want to follow in His steps,
His sacred path we'll trod.
He is not dead. He doth not sleep.
He is the Son of God.

—Larry and Lisa Laycock

Because of their symbolic shape and color, candy canes turn our thoughts to Christ. Our family enjoys decorating our home with candy canes and placing some by our front door either on a tree or in a Christmas bowl to share with anyone who visits during the season. We always try to remember to briefly share our testimony and understanding of the significance of the colors as well as the shape of the little gift.

WHAT YOU CAN DO TO FIND TESTIMONIES OF CHRIST IN THE CANDY CANE

• Provide each family member with a festive candy cane to eat while you have a lesson about how the candy cane testifies of Christ. Testify that Jesus is the Good Shepherd who was willing to die for us, His sheep (see John 10:11). Remember to teach that the white stripes bear record of Christ's purity and that the red stripes bear record of His precious, sacrificial blood. Teach that one of the best messages of the candy cane is that the Good Shepherd speaks words to us that are sweeter than honey (see Psalms 119:103). The sweetness of the candy cane can also remind us that living the gospel should always be a joyful, sweet part of our lives.

• Provide candy canes to family members to be used as decorations for your Christmas tree. As everyone places a candy cane on the tree, explain how the candy bears record of Christ as the Good Shepherd because it is in the shape of a shepherd's crook. Invite all family members to remember Christ whenever they see a candy cane.

- Dish up some candy cane ice cream topped with crushed Oreo cookies and hot fudge sauce. You can also add whipped cream to make it even more festive.

- Make a cup of your favorite hot chocolate. Hang a candy cane over the rim of your mug to infuse your hot chocolate with the delicious candy cane flavor. Enjoy!

Candy Cane Hot Chocolate

INGREDIENTS FOR 1 SERVING
2 cups whole milk

½ cup semisweet and peppermint-flavored chocolate morsels

½ teaspoon red gel, no-taste food coloring

Vanilla sugar whipping cream (see directions below)

DIRECTIONS
In a small pan, combine milk, chocolate morsels, and food coloring. Gently simmer until hot and all chocolate is melted. Pour into a mug, and top with freshly whipped cream. Hang a peppermint candy cane over the mug rim to use for stirring.

Vanilla Sugar Whipped Cream

INGREDIENTS
1 cup heavy whipping cream

2 Tablespoons vanilla sugar (No vanilla sugar? Add regular sugar and a drop of vanilla extract.)

DIRECTIONS
Add heavy cream and vanilla sugar to a cold metal bowl. Either whip by hand with whisk or with hand-held mixer until soft peaks form.

CHAPTER 14

CHRISTMAS COLORS

HOW DO CHRISTMAS COLORS CONFIRM OUR TESTIMONY OF CHRIST?

The colors of Christmas bear record of Jesus Christ by reminding us of His splendor and majesty. White reminds us of Christ's purity. Green symbolizes Christ's gift of eternal life for all mankind. Red bears record of His precious, atoning blood, which was shed for the repentant. Silver and gold signify His royal birthright as the King of kings and Lord of lords. The rich, vibrant colors of Christmas shout praises to our God and King if we pay attention.

When we see beautiful white snow, sparkling white lights, angels dressed in white, or even mounds of creamy white frosting on Christmas delicacies, we can choose to remember the purity of our Savior and how He was able to accomplish the Atonement because of His purity and love. We can choose to follow the Savior by seeking forgiveness for our sins and committing to follow His path of righteousness.

The color green is associated with life and health and the power of nature. Each spring, we are reminded of the renewed cycle of life as the earth turns from pale winter to vibrant living green. When we ponder the deep green of our evergreen trees or the lively green of the wreaths hung on our doors, or even when we watch the bright, shiny green ornaments on our Christmas trees reflect light and create beauty, we can choose to remember that the color green is a constant reminder that the Resurrection of Christ makes everlasting life a reality.

When we embrace the beauty of the color red that surrounds us at Christmastime, we can remember the perfect, priceless gift and sacrifice of our beloved Savior and the blood He freely spilt for us. Deep red sparkling lights shine in the dark and cause the greenery of Christmas to appear even more alive. The red glow of Christmas lights remind us of Christ's life and holy mission to serve as a sacrifice for our sins. They call out our constant need to repent. Red holly berries invite us to think about the drops of blood that Christ shed in Gethsemane, and the crimson ribbon and beautiful red foil paper that envelop our Christmas gifts remind us that Christ's Atonement will cover us completely if we repent and come unto Him.

Finally, the traditional Christmas colors of silver and gold lead our hearts and minds to the understanding that Christ is truly our King. As we delight in the silver and gold that glitter in the lights and decorations of Christmastime, we can choose to see our King in every reflection, on every cup from which we drink, and on each plate from which we feast. The Wise Men brought the precious gift of gold to the Christ child. They knew of His royal lineage and offered their gifts befit for a King. In stark contrast, Judas betrayed Christ with thirty pieces of silver and alienated himself from his best and finest friend. What will we choose to do with the silver and gold of our Christmas celebration? Will they bring us closer to our King, or will they remove us from Him?

The way we choose to see the colors of Christmas will make a difference in how we decide to celebrate Christmas. Our choices also determine what memories we will create for those we love.

WHAT IS THE HISTORY OF CHRISTMAS COLORS?

The colors of Christmas find their origin in both the scriptures and ancient symbolic references to nature. For example, the holy scriptures refer to the color white as a symbol of purity. Isaiah states: "Though your sins be as scarlet, they shall be as white as snow; though they be red like crimson, they shall be as wool" (Isaiah 1:18). The brightness of the sun shining on freshly fallen snow at Christmastime reminds us of all that is pure, clean, and worthy. In winter, snow's blanket of whiteness covers the world and wraps it in a state of spotless beauty that testifies of Christ. Similarly, the white wool that Isaiah describes is a fitting symbol of purity because sheep's wool is not only beautiful to see and touch but also serves many useful purposes, including to clothe and warm. Just as Christ's Atonement can make us clean from every sin, the snow and wool remind us that we can become enveloped in Jesus's love and purity so that we can be useful to God.

"Christmas waves a magic wand over this world, and behold, everything is softer and more beautiful."

—Norman Vincent Peale

The color green is historically associated with all that is eternal and everlasting. In modern times, "going green" is a positive description for respecting all life forms and acting to conserve precious resources. The evergreen tree is properly viewed as a symbol of things that endure and survive even the rigors of cold winter. While other plants fade and die, the evergreen retains its beauty and life through the entire winter season. Green also reminds us of new life. Jesus Christ, through His eternal sacrifice and Resurrection, gives all mankind hope for forgiveness from sin or new life and salvation from death.

The colors gold and silver serve to remind us of Christ's royal and kingly power as well as His celestial glory and incorruptibility. Since ancient times, gold has been sought out as a precious metal. Its resistance to corrosion and

tarnishing coupled with its brilliant, shining appearance make it a highly prized possession. Gold is viewed with such desire and respect that it is considered a valuable currency all over the world. Thus, it is not surprising that Christ's kingship would be honored in the form of that gift. Similarly, the color of silver was anciently associated with the light and power of the moon to influence the tides of the sea. Silver is the color of soothing, sensitivity, and reflection that was believed to change one's direction toward enlightenment and learning. In ancient times, gold and silver were also thought to have medicinal value to heal and purify. Together, the symbolism-rich history of gold and silver point to Christ as the incorruptible and majestic Savior.

The color red represents the blood sacrifice of Jesus Christ. Our Heavenly Father promises that we can be cleansed by the blood of Christ. His blood has been shed for all of us: "This is my blood of the new testament, which is shed for many" (Mark 14:24).

WHAT WE HAVE DONE TO FIND TESTIMONIES OF CHRIST IN CHRISTMAS COLORS

One year near Christmas, we decided to have a family picture taken. On the day of our photo session, we woke up to a fresh blanket of glistening white snow. The sun glittered on the newly fallen snow, and the gorgeous evergreens peeked out from underneath heavy boughs of white. Because we love Christmas colors, we decided to wear red so that the white of the snow would seem even whiter and the red of our clothing would appear even redder. We put on scarves, gloves, coats, and boots and drove into the snow-covered mountains. We sang

Christmas carols and talked about the significance of the red of our clothing and the white of the snow. We pondered how the golden sunlight reminded us of Christ as our King, and we remembered how the evergreen boughs testify to us that because Christ broke the bands of physical death, our lives will not end at death.

When we arrived at the designated spot for our pictures, our photographer had a beautiful Christmas sleigh with shiny silver trim set up for us to use as a backdrop for our photos. It was Christmas at its best! The day was magical for our family. Rather than grumbling and complaining about having to take family pictures, we all enjoyed the beauty of nature, and we remembered our Savior by observing the colors of Christmas. Simply talking about the colors of Christmas brought the Spirit into our hearts, and we thoroughly enjoyed our family gathering. Now, every time we look at those photos, we remember the Christmas colors that focus us on Christ and how everything good is gathered in Him.

WHAT YOU CAN DO TO FIND TESTIMONIES OF CHRIST IN CHRISTMAS COLORS

- Divide the family into five teams, one for each color of Christmas. Hand out pieces of colored paper corresponding to the color for each team—red, green, white, silver, and gold. Have each group list as many Christmas symbols, customs, or items as possible of the color. For example, for the color green, the group might list Christmas tree, wreaths, holly and ivy, garlands, mistletoe, etc.

- Walk through your house together and find as many colors of Christmas as possible. Invite your children to explain how the color can remind us of Christ.

- While driving, shopping, or making visits, see how many Christmas colors you can identify. Recite how each color reminds us of Christ and His sacred mission as Savior of all the world.

- Make some red, green, yellow, and white Christmas Jell-O Jigglers in the shape of Christmas objects. Follow the directions on the box. Use cans of whipping cream to decorate the Jell-O. The family will have fun making and eating this yummy treat. Be sure to discuss the beauty of Christmas colors as you make and eat the Jigglers.

- Prepare an easy, delicious drink that is sure to remind everyone of the symbolism of colors of Christmas.

Christmas Cream

INGREDIENTS

1 carton of sherbet (lime and raspberry are great holiday colors as well as delicious flavors)

2 2-liter bottles of lemon-lime soda

DIRECTIONS

Put sherbet in punch bowl. Add soda, and enjoy!

CHAPTER 15

Holy Family Nativity Scene

HOW DOES THE HOLY FAMILY NATIVITY SCENE CONFIRM OUR TESTIMONY OF CHRIST?

The most essential part of every Nativity scene is a depiction of the Holy Family, which consists of the baby Jesus; His mother, Mary; and His earthly father, Joseph. Larger sets may incorporate shepherds, wise men, angels, a star, and typically a stable or cave including animals that likely shared the stable. Each Nativity scene—whether figures of elaborate hand-carved wood or live children dressed in bathrobes—clearly teaches us of a Holy family and a sacred birth. The Holy Family focuses our thoughts on Heavenly Father's love for us by reminding us that we belong to His holy family and that we have an earthly family that can also become holy. John the Beloved taught, "For God so loved the world that He gave His only begotten son, that whosoever believeth in Him should not perish, but have everlasting life" (John 3:16).

The first Christmas decorations our family displays each season are our Nativity scenes. We think of Christ when we display them because they remind us of His humble coming into the world in fulfillment of God's promise to provide a Savior for all mankind. When we use Nativity scenes to teach our family that Heavenly Father kept His promise to provide a Savior, we increase the trust we feel that God will continue to protect and bless us. Throughout history, Heavenly Father has inspired His prophets to teach and tell the story of the Nativity. It was Isaiah who foretold Christ's birth more than seven hundred years before the event (see Isaiah 9:6). Other prophets and teachers join Isaiah in testifying that the advent of Jesus's birth demonstrates that God loves all His children.

The Gospel of Luke presents an intimate description of the Nativity scene anticipated by the writings of Isaiah, stating, "And she brought forth her firstborn son, and wrapped him in swaddling clothes, and laid him in a manger; because there was no room for them in the inn" (Luke 2:7).

When we pay attention to the full significance of the traditional Nativity scene—especially the Holy Family—we come to know that a Nativity set is not just a decoration that depicts where baby Jesus rested on the night of His birth. Rather, the Nativity scene is a sign to all faithful seekers of Christ. It reminds us to heed the counsel and prophesying of prophets and to listen carefully to God's messengers in order to obtain eternal life. The traditional Nativity scene also serves to remind us that God will *again* keep His promise as His prophets have foretold: Christ will return to the earth as Lord of lords and King of kings.

WHAT IS THE HISTORY OF THE NATIVITY SCENE?

The Nativity scene is referred to by many names such as crèche, crib, *pesebre*, *presepio*, *krippe*, and *nacimiento*, but a depiction of the birth of Jesus Christ is common to all such scenes. Not all Nativities are completely accurate or consistent with the details in the Bible. Nevertheless, Nativity scenes help us remember essential events surrounding the birth of Christ.

Saint Francis of Assisi is believed to have created the first "Nativity scene," in which he arranged for a "living" depiction of the birth of Christ. In about 1223, in a cave near Greccio, Italy, Saint Francis made arrangements to present a living model of what the birth of Christ was believed to have been like. He hoped to emphasize worship of Christ and draw attention away from secular practices at Christmastime. Saint Francis intended to encourage not only the worship of Christ but also a deeper understanding of the significance of His birth. With the approval of ecclesiastical leaders, the "living" Nativity scene became popular, and soon people throughout all Christendom began to present Nativity displays.

"For unto us a child is born, unto us a son is given: and the government shall be upon his shoulder: and his name shall be called Wonderful, Counsellor, The mighty God, The everlasting Father, The Prince of Peace."

—Isaiah 9:6

The brief and often personal and intimate descriptions written by Matthew and Luke provide a clear understanding of the events of the night of our Savior's birth. It appears that Luke found access to intimate information about the birth of Christ because Luke apparently accompanied Paul during his interview of James the brother of Jesus (see Acts 21:18). Gospel scholars also note that during Paul's confinement after arrest in the temple, Luke could have remained in the Holy Land and thus interviewed eyewitnesses to

the life and ministry of Jesus, including Jesus's mother, Mary, who might still have been alive. In this way, Luke could have learned of the stories about Jesus's conception, birth, and childhood."[10] It is highly probable that through such interviews, Luke came to know what treasures Mary kept and "pondered in her heart" (Luke 2:19, 51).

WHAT WE HAVE DONE TO FIND TESTIMONIES OF CHRIST IN THE NATIVITY SCENE

Years ago, our family decided to make it a tradition to find ourselves in the Nativity each season. We have learned to more fully appreciate and love our Savior as we have helped our family members ponder how they can all find themselves in the Nativity and life of our Savior. For example, one year, I (Lisa) decided to see myself as Mary during the Christmas season. I studied Mary's life. I tried to think like Mary would think. As I planned Christmas that year, I found testimonies of Christ in unusual places and diverse situations because I was striving to think, speak, and act as Mary would. This activity is always a powerful experience for our family.

---

10 Richard N. Holazpfel, Eric D. Huntsman, and Thomas A. Wayment, *Jesus Christ and the World of the New Testament*, (2007), 110.

WHAT YOU CAN DO TO FIND TESTIMONIES OF CHRIST IN THE NATIVITY SCENE

- Set aside a particular day in late November or early December to engage in the yearly tradition of setting up your family Nativity scene. We use the day after Thanksgiving. Make it a meaningful event, and take time to savor the activity. Discuss each element of the Nativity and how it bears record of Christ as you reverently place your display. Once your Nativity scene is in place, you may want to invite family members to find themselves in the Nativity scene during the Christmas season. For example, you can find yourself in the shepherds as you do missionary work, sharing your witness of the reality of Christ and giving care and guidance to the Great Pastor's flock. As you sing Christmas hymns, you can find yourself in the "multitude of the heavenly host praising God, and saying, Glory to God in the highest, and on earth peace, good will toward men" (Luke 2:13–14). You can find yourself in the Wise Men as you or family members leave the comforts of home and family to serve others. You might want to invite family members to prepare to testify of their experience on Christmas Eve or Christmas Day. This can be a powerful spiritual activity. Family testimonies will sweetly bear record of Jesus in previously unobserved ways. You may want to video-record your family testimonies for future reference.

- You could dress up young children as people in the Nativity scene. Take pictures, and use the pictures for your family Christmas card. One year, we dressed our three young grandsons as Wise Men and printed the photo on a Christmas card with the words: Wise Men and Women Still Seek Him. Our family and friends loved receiving the special, personal card.

- A fun, yet meaningful family Nativity activity is to create chocolate molds of the Holy Family to eat or to share with family and friends.

- One fun and interactive Christmas tradition helps families focus on giving, the true meaning of Christmas, and the spirit of service. It includes a manger, straw, and a baby Jesus. Each time a family member completes an act of service a piece of straw is placed in the manger. On Christmas day the baby Jesus is placed in the manger that has been filled with service and love. Such a set, called the Giving Manger, is available for purchase at www.the-givingmanger.com.

Holy Family Chocolate Pieces

Purchase a mold of the Holy Family and some melting chocolates of different colors and flavors.

Melt the chocolate, being careful not to let it burn. For us it works best to melt it in the microwave. Others prefer a double boiler.

Carefully pour the chocolate into the mold.

Cool in refrigerator or let stand at room temperature until hardened.

When solid, remove chocolates from mold.

Be sure to discuss the Holy Family while making and enjoying these special chocolate treats!

CHAPTER 16

SHEPHERDS

HOW DO CHRISTMAS SHEPHERDS CONFIRM OUR TESTIMONY OF CHRIST?

After the birth of Christ, the angel of the Lord appeared to shepherds who were keeping watch over their flock. The angel gave them a sign by which they could identify their Savior: "And this shall be a sign unto you; Ye shall find the babe wrapped in swaddling clothes, lying in a manger" (Luke 2:12). Shepherds are almost always present in Nativity scenes, and rightly so. The shepherds came in "haste" on the evening of Jesus's birth "and found Mary, and Joseph, and the babe lying in a manger" (Luke 2:16). The statements "let us now go even unto Bethlehem, and see this thing which is come to pass, which the Lord hath made known unto us" and "they came with haste" demonstrate the shepherds' urgent determination to find the Christ child (Luke 2:15–16).

Shepherds bear record of Christ in at least four ways:

First, the shepherds help us to remember Jesus's declaration: "I am the Good Shepherd" (see John 10:11–14). The shepherd image reminds us that Christ will watch over, protect, and guide us as we come unto Him and become members of His flock. The beautiful imagery of His example teaches us that we are the sheep or followers of a loving Shepherd who will guide us to the fold of His everlasting gospel. As the Good Shepherd, the Savior provides spiritual guidance and protection from evil and temptation. He always searches for His lost sheep and carries them back to His fold through His infinite Atonement and love (see Luke 15:1–7).

Second, the shepherds help us to remember that Jesus, the Good Shepherd, charges us with caring for and nourishing His sheep. Responding to the resurrected Christ's three inquiries as to whether or not Peter loved Him, the chief Apostle said "Lord, thou knowest all things; thou knowest that I love thee" (John 21:17). Christ then explains that we, like Peter, can show our love for Him by nourishing and caring for others. He instructed Peter simply and concisely, "Feed my sheep" (John 21:17). As with Peter, Jesus asks us to show our godly love by nourishing, caring for, and watching over His flock (see John 21:15–17). The symbol of the shepherd prompts us to be like our Savior, who is our loving, caring Good Shepherd.

Third, the shepherds in our Nativity scenes remind us of Luke's account of the shepherds at Christ's birth. We remember that we can be like these humble believers, worthy to receive the heavenly manifestation of concourses of angels who announced the birth of the Savior. The shepherds teach us how we should respond when we receive truth. Like the shepherds, we

"And there were in the same country shepherds abiding in the field, keeping watch over their flock by night. And, lo, the angel of the Lord came upon them, and the glory of the Lord shone round about them: and they were sore afraid. And the angel said unto them, Fear not: for, behold, I bring you good tidings of great joy, which shall be to all people. For unto you is born this day in the city of David a Saviour, which is Christ the Lord. And this shall be a sign unto you; Ye shall find the babe wrapped in swaddling clothes, lying in a manger."

—Luke 2:8–12

can go in haste to find, serve, and worship Jesus. They did not delay or debate. They did not worry or wait.

The shepherds may have known the Messiah was to be born in Bethlehem. Old Testament scriptures foretold that Christ's birth would indeed occur there. In the book of Micah, we read:

"But thou, Bethlehem Ephratah, though thou be little among the thousands of Judah, yet out of thee shall he come forth unto me that is to be ruler in Israel; whose goings forth have been from of old, from everlasting. Therefore will he give them up, until the time that she which travaileth hath brought forth: then the remnant of his brethren shall return unto the children of Israel. And he shall stand and feed in the strength of the Lord, in the majesty of the name of the Lord his God; and they shall abide: for now shall he be great unto the ends of the earth" (Micah 5:2–4).

It is also possible that the shepherds understood and interpreted the writings in Micah 4:8 as a revelation foretelling the coming of the Messiah at the "tower of the flock," a place referred to in the scriptures as "Migdal Eder," which is in the town of Bethlehem. In Genesis, we learn that Rachel was buried on the way to Ephrath—that is, Bethlehem (see Genesis 35:19–21). It was in this place of the tower of the flock that the scriptures foretell as the place where "dominion shall come" (Micah 4:8).

And so, after being visited by angels near the tower of the flock, the shepherds made their way with all possible speed to the place where the sign of a babe wrapped in swaddling clothes and lying in a manger would confirm the birth of their Messiah.

Finally, the shepherds in our Nativity scenes remind us of our calling to share our knowledge of Christ with the world. After witnessing the child lying in a manger, the shepherds became messengers of Christ's birth; they happily shared their testimony with all who would hear them. Like the shepherds of old, we too may bear record of Christ, and declare His gospel to all.

WHAT IS THE HISTORY OF CHRISTMAS SHEPHERDS?

During the meridian of time, when Christ was born, those who lived in and around Jerusalem relied on sheep for many important necessities of life. Sheep were a significant source of food and clothing. Shepherds always maintained careful watch to protect the valued flock.

The shepherds in our Christmas celebrations are humble followers of Christ. They are examples of simple faith and obedience. They teach us to rush to find and worship Christ. They inspire us to feed His sheep, protect His flocks, and stand as witnesses of Christ.

WHAT WE HAVE DONE TO FIND TESTIMONIES OF CHRIST IN CHRISTMAS SHEPHERDS

In our family, we consider swaddling clothes to be the first Christmas pajamas. When we were newly married and looking forward to celebrating our first Christmas together, we discovered that both of our families had a common tradition: Christmas pajamas. We had enjoyed receiving Christmas pajamas each year of our childhood, and we decided that we wanted to continue the fun Christmas pajama tradition in our own family. We then realized that the pajama tradition could take on a special meaning if we thought of it in terms of the sign God gave the shepherds to identify the Christ child, who would be "wrapped in swaddling clothes and lying in a manger." We began to use our treasured Christmas pajama tradition to remind us of the importance of following the signs that lead to Christ.

If you continue the tradition of wearing special Christmas pajamas each year, we invite you to testify that all of us can become like the humble shepherds of old who searched out and followed the signs of Christ's coming.

WHAT YOU CAN DO TO FIND TESTIMONIES OF CHRIST IN CHRISTMAS SHEPHERDS

- Distribute special Christmas pajamas to your family members. You could design a treasure hunt and allow the children to search for them. Or you could have the pajamas specially wrapped and under your Christmas tree. Be creative in how you distribute them. Explain that the Christmas pajamas have a special symbolic significance: they remind us of the swaddling clothes of the baby Jesus on the night of His birth. Your kids will never tire of this fun and inspiring activity. Even if you do it year after year, they will still look forward to it. Discuss the blessings that can come from following the example of the shepherds, who went with haste to find Christ and testify of His life and teachings.

- Sing with your family "Angels We Have Heard On High," and help your family imagine what it would have been like to be a shepherd who witnessed the choir of angels singing praises to the newborn King.

- Gather your family, and ask family members, "How would you feel and what would you do in response to the experience that the shepherds had?" Write or video-record each family member as he or she expresses his or her feelings. Watching these recorded testimonies each year can become a treasured family Christmas tradition. As time passes, children, children-in-law, and grandchildren will look forward to the yearly viewing of these dear Christmas testimonies and memories.

- As a family, make Christmas bread, form it in the shape of a shepherd's crook, and bake it. Eat it with honey butter and cold milk as you discuss the mission of the shepherds. Or go caroling to a neighbor's home. Leave the bread and a message about the shepherds and how they testify of Christ.

- Make and pull Christmas taffy as a family. Shape the taffy into shepherd's crooks. Then enjoy eating as you read about the shepherds in Luke 2. Discuss how the shepherds bear witness of Christ.

Shepherd's Crook Taffy

INGREDIENTS

1¼ cups corn syrup

1 cup sugar

1 Tablespoon water

1 Tablespoon white vinegar

1 teaspoon butter

½ teaspoon vanilla or mint extract

Food coloring as desired

DIRECTIONS

Put all ingredients in a large saucepan. Stir to combine. Place candy thermometer on side of pan and bring to a boil. Stir to prevent burning. Cook to firm-ball or hard-ball stage (225 degrees). Remove from heat. Stir in desired extract and food coloring, and pour onto baking sheet lined with wax paper or silicone baking sheet. Let mixture cool just enough to handle it. Roll into a log and stretch or pull the taffy to work air into it. Pull and stretch as you fold it over and over until it becomes opaque. Continue pulling and twisting until it starts to harden. Before it is completely hardened, cut and mold it into the shape of a shepherd's crook. Lay pieces on wax paper to set.

Be sure to laugh and talk as you stretch and shape the taffy.

HELPFUL TIPS

Oil the top inch of saucepan wall to keep sugar from boiling over.

Use a bigger pan than you think you need to prevent boiling over.

Use a burner as big as or bigger than your pan bottom.

Don't scrape bottom of pan when finished cooking taffy, just pour out syrup.

Butter hands before stretching. This keeps taffy from sticking to hands.

Wash down sides of pan with a clean wet pastry brush during cooking to avoid crystallization of sugar.

CHAPTER 17

CHRISTMAS ANIMALS

HOW DO CHRISTMAS ANIMALS CONFIRM OUR TESTIMONY OF CHRIST?

Our family enjoys relating the beautiful legends surrounding Christmas animals each year. In the telling and retelling of these legends, we find both witnesses and testimonies of Christ and His mission. It is not clear exactly which animals were actually present at the time of Jesus's birth, but many beautiful animal legends have grown out of the recounting of the Nativity story. One legend recounts that cattle knelt to adore the Christ child on the eve of His birth, and thus they continue to be a domestic animal that kneels before lying down. The donkey shared the journey of Joseph and the expectant Mary, carrying Mary and the unborn child over the many miles of difficult travel. The cross that appears on a donkey's back is thought to be a symbol of humble service and a foreshadowing of Christ bearing our burdens on the cross of Calvary. Even the prophet Isaiah pays homage to these Christmas animals: "The ox knoweth his owner, and the ass his master's crib" (Isaiah 1:3).

Sheep and lambs certainly have their part in the story, along with their shepherds. The angel of the Lord appears to the shepherds abiding in the field, keeping watch over their flock (see Luke 2:8–9). The referenced flock must have witnessed the angelic visitation as well—"the glory of the Lord shone round about them" (Luke 2:9). Christ is both referred to as and calls Himself the Good Shepherd and the Lamb of God. "And looking upon Jesus as he walked, he saith, Behold the Lamb of God!" (John 1:36). "I am the good shepherd: the good shepherd giveth his life for the sheep" (John 10:11).

In the stable at Jesus's birth, we expect that other animals were present, including the domestic animals of the day along with songbirds and doves. Among the many beautiful legends, one explains that the robin's red breast gained its color by steadfastly fanning the flames of the fire used to warm the baby Jesus until its feathers turned the color of the red-hot coals. Another story explains that the songbirds, such as the dove, used their songs to soothe the resting child in the stable. In the Philippines, Spain, and many Latin American countries, the observance of the *Misa del Gallo,* or the midnight Mass of the Rooster, recounts the legend that on the night of Jesus's birth, the rooster crowed at midnight, signaling the appearance of a bright light that accompanied the birth of the Son of God: "In [Jesus] was life; and the life was the light of men. And the light shineth in darkness" (John 1:4–5).

"Behold the Lamb of God, which taketh away the sin of the world."

—John 1:29

There is another ancient legend that explains that on Christmas Eve, animals are given the power to speak in order to commemorate that it was so on the night of our Savior's birth. As part of the legend, all mortals are warned not to listen to the voices of the animals in order to avoid mishap.

The tradition of sharing these stories helps us bear record of Jesus Christ as we remember how animals witnessed Christ's first coming into the world. We use these animals as examples of loving kindness and service. We use animal shapes for cookies and as ornaments to decorate Christmas cards and to adorn our Christmas Nativities.

WHAT IS THE HISTORY OF CHRISTMAS ANIMALS?

The exact origins of Christmas animal legends are not clear, but a clue is found in the ancient practice of telling the Nativity story in song so that the illiterate believers of the past would remember the story of Christ's birth. One such medieval traditional English

song explains the role of Christmas animals from the perspective of the "friendly beasts." Although the author is unknown, the clear reverence for our Savior as our kind and good brother is unmistakable in the "Carol of the Friendly Beasts":

Carol of the Friendly Beasts

Jesus, our brother, kind and good,
Was humbly born in a stable rude;
And the friendly beasts around him stood,
Jesus, our brother, kind and good.

"I," said the donkey, shaggy and brown,
"I carried his mother up-hill and down,
I carried her safely to Bethlehem town."
"I," said the donkey, shaggy and brown.

"I," said the cow, all white and red,
"I gave him my manger for a bed,
I gave him my hay to pillow his head."
"I," said the cow, all white and red.

"I," said the sheep with the curly horn,
"I gave him my wool for a blanket warm,
He wore my coat on Christmas morn."
"I," said the sheep with the curly horn.

"I," said the dove from the rafters high,
"I cooed him to sleep so he would not cry,
We cooed him to sleep, my mate and I."
"I," said the dove from the rafters high.

Jesus, our brother, kind and good,
Was humbly born in a stable rude;
And the friendly beasts around him stood,
Jesus, our brother, kind and good.

As we ponder the animals that help us celebrate Christmas, we also remember that Jesus Christ is the great creator of all things: "All things were made by him; and without him was not any thing made that was made" (John 1:3). These songs, stories, and legends reach out across the centuries and create living testimonies of the Savior and His love for all of His creations.

WHAT WE HAVE DONE TO FIND TESTIMONIES OF CHRIST IN CHRISTMAS ANIMALS

We have carefully collected animal pieces for the Nativity sets in our home over the thirty-five years of our marriage. The collection has come to include donkeys, oxen, sheep, lambs, camels ridden by the Magi, and at some point even some small pigs made their way into one of our Nativity sets. Each year as we explained the stories surrounding the animals, inevitably our children moved the creatures of each set into close circles around the small mangers. This innocent act taught us the important lesson that each individual can contribute to service in Christ's kingdom here on earth. No matter how small or seemingly insignificant their contribution, those who serve and worship Christ will find their way into the circle of servants that surround Him. We reminisce about how each animal used its own unique strengths and abilities to serve the Holy Family. Together we learned from the example of the Christmas animals how we should likewise search among our own abilities and strengths and seek to serve our Savior with our own unique gifts and abilities. Our collection of Christmas animals reminds us that Jesus Christ is the Author of all creation and that all living creatures deserve our respect and reverence.

WHAT YOU CAN DO TO FIND TESTIMONIES OF CHRIST IN CHRISTMAS ANIMALS

- Gather together and visit a living Nativity experience. As you pass by the live animals, talk about the individual animals, what their unique talents or gifts might be, and what their service is in the story of the Nativity.

- Begin a Christmas animal collection for your family. Add at least one special animal for the Nativity or as ornaments to decorate your Christmas tree. Discuss the animals that may have participated in the events of the first Christmas season and how they might have used their special or unique talents or gifts to serve. Invite your family members to share a unique gift that they possess and to find a way to use it to serve others during the Christmas season.

- Dip animal crackers into Cookie Dough Dip. Enjoy the cookies or give them as a gift along with a short explanation of the testimony of the Christmas animals. Over the years, our family has enjoyed making this yummy dip and then dipping animal crackers into it as we have discussed the significance of and the legends of Christmas animals and how they carry our thoughts to Christ and His birth and life.

Cookie Dough Dip

INGREDIENTS

½ cup butter (room temperature)

8 ounces cream cheese

⅓ cup light brown sugar

½ cup powdered sugar

Pinch of salt

1 teaspoon vanilla extract

1 teaspoon ground cinnamon

1 teaspoon ground nutmeg

¾ cup chocolate chips

DIRECTIONS

In electric mixer, cream the butter and cream cheese until fluffy. On low speed, add the rest of the ingredients except chocolate chips, and mix thoroughly. Fold in chocolate chips. Can be refrigerated until ready to serve, but needs to be at room temperature for dipping animal crackers.

CHAPTER 18

WISE MEN (MAGI)

HOW DO THE WISE MEN CONFIRM OUR TESTIMONY OF CHRIST?

The magi, or Wise Men, always form an important part of the Nativity scene. We revere and remember them for their ability to see and follow the star of the "King of the Jews" (Matthew 2:2). We also remember them as the givers of good gifts. In the words of O. Henry in his classic Christmas tale "The Gift of the Magi": "The magi, as you know, were wise men—wonderfully wise men who brought gifts to the Babe in the manger. They invented the art of giving Christmas presents." The Wise Men remind us to give our best gifts to Christ.

Upon their arrival in Jerusalem, they explained that they had followed a star all the way to Jerusalem to worship the newborn King. These majestic men's visit troubled King Herod, who promptly demanded that the chief priest and scribes search the prophecies so that he could know the place of Christ's birth (see Matthew 2:3–4). The priests and scribes revealed the prophetic birthplace as Bethlehem (see Matthew 2:5–6; see also Micah 5:2).

In a false attempt at sincerity, Herod sent the Wise Men in search of the newborn King, demanding that they send him word so that he too could go and worship (see Matthew 2:7–8). After leaving Herod's presence, the Wise Men followed the star until they found the young Jesus. Rejoicing, they fell down and worshiped Him and opened their treasures to Him (see Matthew 2:9–11).

Just as God warned Joseph in a dream to protect his little family by fleeing into Egypt, God instructed the Wise Men *not* to return to Herod (see Matthew 2:12–14). God instructed them to "go home another way."

In thoughtful contemplation of the story of the magi and their interaction with both Herod and Christ, we remember that we must ignore the demands of worldly influences that seek to destroy Christ, His church, and the family. In the process of searching for Christ, we too will encounter those who feign allegiance to Jesus but actually represent the destructive forces of Satan. Like the Wise Men, we must reject the evil powers and influences of the Herods of this world. We must pursue the promptings of the Holy Spirit that guide us home "another way."

Charles Dickens expresses the importance of avoiding the darkness of worldly influence in *A Christmas Carol*. Through the character of Marley's Ghost, who responds to Scrooge's observance that Marley was always a good man of business, Dickens explains: "Business! . . . Mankind was my business. The common welfare was my business; charity, mercy, forbearance, and benevolence, were, all, my business. The dealings of my trade were but a drop of water in the comprehensive

"Now when Jesus was born in Bethlehem of Judea in the days of Herod the King, behold, there came wise men from the east to Jerusalem, Saying Where is he that is born King of the Jews? For we have seen his star in the east, and are come to worship him."

—Matthew 2:1–2

ocean of my business! . . . Why did I walk through crowds of fellow-beings with my eyes turned down, and never raise them to that blessed star which led the Wise Men to a poor abode? Were there no poor homes to which its light would have conducted me?"[11]

It is up to us to make mankind and the common welfare our daily pursuit. It is incumbent upon every man and woman to look upward to the "blessed star which led the Wise Men to a poor abode" and find the home to which the star's guiding light will conduct us. As we do so, the Christmas star will remind us to seek Christ diligently by serving our fellow man.

WHAT IS THE HISTORY OF THE WISE MEN?

A careful review of the Gospel accounts of the birth of Christ reveals that the Wise Men were not present on the night of the Savior's birth; however, the typical Nativity scene includes three Wise Men. Matthew explains that the Wise Men actually visited the "young child with Mary his mother" when they "were come into the house" (Matthew 2:11). Though it is not known how many Wise Men there were, they are traditionally thought to be a trio. This is based upon the number of gifts presented to Jesus when they "fell down, and worshipped him" (Matthew 2:11).

Our knowledge of the Wise Men comes exclusively from the scriptural account. Although the scriptures provide limited information concerning who they are and whence they came, we do know that they were spiritually directed and inspired. We also know that they received guidance from spiritual sources and followed that direction—whether in the form of the star or in dreams. The reference to the Wise Men as magi may refer to their status as physicians, seers, priests, or teachers. We do not know exactly what their backgrounds may have been, but we can trust that they had a prophetic vision of the Savior, that they were true worshipers of Christ, and that they braved an arduous journey in order to bestow valuable and meaningful gifts upon Him.

---

11 Charles Dickens, *A Christmas Carol*, London: Bradbury and Evans, Printers, Whitefriars (1843), 8–9.

The gift of myrrh represents the enabling Atonement of the Savior. Myrrh is a soothing ointment used to treat and heal wounds and alleviate pain and suffering. Frankincense is an aromatic resin used in both burned incense and in perfumes, and it symbolizes communication with God, as the smoke of the incense symbolically rises to heaven. Because the smoke rises from ashes, the frankincense also represents the Resurrection of Jesus in His risen state as a glorified physical being. Finally, the gold is a kingly or royal gift given to the King of kings. Gold also represents purity and incorruptibility, symbolizing Christ's perfect, sinless example. The gifts that the Wise Men brought should serve to remind us of the first gift of Christmas: Heavenly Father's gift of His Son to the world. The Wise Men's gifts may also remind us of Christ's gifts to us: His sinless life, His infinite Atonement, and our salvation from sin and death. The gifts of the magi clearly symbolize these heavenly gifts and testify of the holy mission of our Savior.

WHAT WE HAVE DONE TO FIND TESTIMONIES OF CHRIST IN THE WISE MEN

One snowy Christmas Eve years ago, we sat on the floor of our family room by the glow of the warm coals in the fireplace, reading some of our favorite Christmas stories. As we read O. Henry's "Gift of the Magi," we talked about how the best Christmas gifts are usually those that require little expense, some sacrifice, and lots of love. In the story, a young married couple finds a way to demonstrate their love for one another by giving personal gifts that require significant personal sacrifice. Our youngest daughter was greatly troubled by the ending of the story because due to their sacrifices, the young couple is unable to use their Christmas gifts. We explained that it is the *giving* of gifts that creates beautiful memories and helps to change us for the better and find true satisfaction at Christmastime. By sacrificing and giving of our time and talents, we show real love and compassion, and at the same time, we serve God. We find true joy in giving gifts like the Wise Men and like our Heavenly Father, who lovingly gave us the gift of His only begotten Son.

With this story as a backdrop, our family conducted a Christmas Eve event where we made homemade gifts that took sacrifice of either money or time or both. When we shared the gifts, we talked about the gifts of the magi and the importance of giving our best gifts of time, sincere kindness, and love to our fellow man and to Christ.

WHAT YOU CAN DO TO FIND TESTIMONIES OF CHRIST IN THE WISE MEN

- Conduct a family activity in early December in which each family member prepares a written promise to give a gift of service to someone they care about that will take some sacrifice during the holiday season. You may want to place the written promises in a beautiful gift box near the Wise Men in your Nativity set. On or after Christmas, open the beautiful gift box containing the written promises to give a gift of service, and tell one another about your experiences as you gave meaningful service to others.

- Follow the Spanish tradition of carrying lamps through the streets of your neighborhood on Christmas Eve. The lamps represent the light of the Star of Bethlehem that shows wise men and women the path to our Savior. Allow each family member to carry a flashlight or lantern, and while walking through your neighborhood, discuss the difficult journey of the Wise Men who followed the Christmas star.

- When our children were very young, they enjoyed helping the Wise Men journey to Christ. To do so, place the three Wise Men a distance away from the Nativity set. Each day before Christmas, help the young children move the Wise Men closer to the stable where Joseph, Mary, and the baby Jesus are found. The goal is to help your children move the Wise Men so that they will arrive on Christmas day in order to present their gifts to Jesus. Discuss the Wise Men and their journey toward the baby Jesus each day leading up to Christmas. Liken the journey of the Wise Men to our life's journey and the path we walk toward eternal life. We must obey and endure to the end in order to find Jesus.

- Bake some brownies topped with thick fudge icing and sprinkles that look like jewels that the Wise Men might have worn or carried. Don't forget a tall glass of cold milk. Discuss the Wise Men and their role in testifying of Christ.

Wise Man Brownies

INGREDIENTS

 2 cups flour

 2 cups sugar

 ½ teaspoon salt

 1 cup shortening

 1 cup water

 3 Tablespoons cocoa

 2 eggs

 1 teaspoon baking soda

 ½ cup buttermilk

 1 teaspoon vanilla

DIRECTIONS

Combine flour, sugar, and salt in a bowl. Combine shortening, water, and cocoa in a saucepan, and bring to a boil; pour over flour mixture. In another bowl, beat eggs, baking soda, buttermilk, and vanilla. Add to flour and cocoa mixture, and mix well. Bake at 350 degrees for 25 minutes.

Frosting

INGREDIENTS

   ½ cup butter

   3 Tablespoons cocoa

   6 Tablespoons milk

   1 pound powdered sugar

   1 teaspoon vanilla

   ½ cup chopped nuts (optional)

DIRECTIONS

   Melt butter in pan with the cocoa. Add milk, powdered sugar, vanilla, and chopped nuts. Mix until creamy. Spread on cool brownies. Top with sprinkles that remind you of the jewels the magi would have owned.

Gold, Frankincense, and Myrrh Snacks

   Fill special containers that look like the Wise Men's gift boxes with candied almonds and pecans that look like bits of frankincense and myrrh. Fill another box with popcorn to look like chunks of gold. Talk about the gifts that the Wise Men gave Christ and discuss how the Wise Men bear record of Christ and inspire us to give our most precious gifts to our Savior.

Candied Almonds

INGREDIENTS

  1 cup sugar

  1 teaspoon ground cinnamon

  1 teaspoon salt

  2 Tablespoons butter

  ¼ cup water

  3 cups raw, whole almonds

DIRECTIONS

  In a large frying pan or pot, combine all ingredients except nuts over medium heat until sugar dissolves. Add almonds; stir constantly until mixture crystallizes (8–10 minutes). Move from pan to serving dish or parchment paper and allow to cool before serving.

Candied Pecans

INGREDIENTS

  1 cup sugar

  1 teaspoon ground cinnamon

  1 teaspoon salt

  2 Tablespoons butter

  Raw, whole pecans

DIRECTIONS

  Follow the same directions as almonds, except add pecans instead of almonds.

  The popcorn can symbolize gold. The almonds will resemble frankincense. And the pecans will look like bits of myrrh. We like to munch on these goodies while we talk about the gifts the Wise Men brought the baby Jesus, and our whole house smells like the scrumptious holiday treat.

CONCLUSION

Christmas is clearly a time to gather sweet family memories and strengthen individual testimonies of Jesus Christ. We invite you to gather your family and friends in the warm spirit of Christmas and joyfully seek Christ in each of your traditions, customs, and keepsakes.

Through our life's experiences, we have come to know that it is definitely possible to overlook the testimonies of Christ that can be found in our Christmas customs and traditions. If we simply hand down fun activities from generation to generation without paying attention to how they testify of Christ, we will miss out on the rich symbolism that is inherent in the sweet celebration of Christmas. In fact, if we're not careful, we could actually celebrate Christmas without ever seeking Christ!

We testify that if you choose to patiently plan your Christmas activities, having eyes to see and ears to hear, you will uncover in them rich, hidden testimonies of our Savior. You will be content to linger among the cherished sights, smells, and sounds of Christmas. You will become a true Christmas disciple. And you will always seek Christ in your celebration of Christmas. We promise that these testimonies will enhance your relationships, fill your hearts with charity, and teach you how to become more like our Savior and our Heavenly Father.